THEN AND THERE SERIES
GENERAL EDITOR
MARJORIE REEVES, M.A., PH.D.

Edwin Chadwick, Poor Law and Public Health

ROGER WATSON

Illustrated from contemporary sources

LONGMAN

LONGMAN GROUP LIMITED
London

Associated companies, branches and representatives
throughout the world

First published 1969
Third impression 1971

ISBN 0 582 20458 5

Printed in Hong Kong by
Wing Tai Cheung Printing Co Ltd

FOR PAT

Acknowledgements
The author is grateful to the following for permission to consult and quote from local
records: The Archivist, Ipswich and East Suffolk Record Office, County Hall, Ipswich
for material in Chapter 4 and The Medical Officer of Health and Corporation of
Darlington for material in Chapter 8. He also owes a considerable debt to S. E. Finer's
biography *The Life and Times of Edwin Chadwick* (Methuen).

The author and publisher are grateful to the following for permission to reproduce
photographs: Aerofilms, page 46; Illustrated London News, page 65; the Archivist
Ipswich and East Suffolk Record Office, pages 30, 34, 40 and 41; Punch, page 71
(cartoon by Leech); Radio Times Hulton Picture Library, pages 1, 4, 6, 8, 11(2), 16,
18, 20, 22, 24, 35(2), 48, 49, 62, 63, 66, 73, 75, 76, 93 and 95; Sunderland Museum and
Art Gallery, page 70; the Wellcome Trustees, pages 51, 52, 54, 56(2) and 58.

Contents

To the Reader

Today, in Britain, if you are out of work because of sickness or because there are no jobs, the Government will pay you a weekly allowance until you get a job again. Throughout much of the nineteenth century you would probably have had to go into a workhouse, or starve. This was the result of the Poor Law Amendment Act (1834).

Today, in Britain, nearly all towns have good roads, proper drains, water supply, public parks and baths. Most houses have running water and flushing toilets, and dustmen take away the rubbish. In the 1830s and 1840s no towns and very few houses had all this. The improvements began with the Health of Towns Act (1848).

Both these Acts were largely the result of the work of one man—Edwin Chadwick. He probably did more to affect the daily life of working people in the nineteenth century than any other man. We owe a great deal to him, but in his time he was known as the most hated man in England. He was hated by the working classes for the New Poor Law under which they suffered. He was hated by many of the wealthier classes for the Public Health Act because they had to pay for the improvements which were made under it.

This book is about Chadwick's career and the workings of these two important Acts.

1 Chadwick's Early Life

Chadwick's Character

In 1928 Chadwick's daughter Marion was asked to say what her father was like. This is what she wrote: 'Whatever may have been his faults, harsh, gloomy and severe he certainly was not.

Edwin Chadwick

To understand him one must remember that he belonged to a generation which was working its way out of the barbarism of former ages. The Reformers of those days were so much absorbed in the tasks they had undertaken that they had hardly any thoughts for the minor details of social and domestic life, and my father was an extreme example of that type. Being somewhat passionate and *fanatical** he looked on those who disagreed with him as enemies of humanity. This made him many enemies but also many warm friends amongst those who respected the genuineness of his convictions.'

This gives us a good idea of Chadwick's character. At a time when most people were prepared to accept situations as they were, Chadwick was determined to change them. He looked at the terrible conditions of life for working people and decided that they were not necessary. Dirt, disease, and the inefficient Poor Laws wasted years of peoples' lives. His life was devoted to changing this situation.

But he cannot have been an easy man to work with. He had no sense of humour and little understanding of other people. He was very sensitive to criticism, but he worked long hours and had an amazing ability to study a confused situation and then come up with a complete plan of reform. Once he had decided on a plan he fought for it against all opposition. This made him many enemies and eventually they were too much for him.

His Early Life

Little is known about Chadwick's early days or about his private life. He was born in 1800 at Longsight near Manchester. While he was still a small boy his mother died, his father's business failed and his father decided to move to London to become a journalist. In London, Chadwick's father remarried and in 1812 became Editor of 'The Statesman'. Chadwick did not go to school in London but was educated at home by his father and by private tutors. We know that he must have been good at modern languages because in later life Chadwick could speak French almost as well as English.

2   *Words printed in *italics* are listed in the glossary on p. 99.

In 1816 his father was offered the job of editor of 'The Western Times' and moved to Devon with his family. Chadwick, however, decided not to go with them and stayed in London. At the age of 18 he made up his mind to become an *attorney*. This would have meant seven years of apprenticeship, and in fact he worked the next five years as an attorney's clerk. But by then his ambitions had grown. Attorneys held the lowest rank in the legal profession. Their job was to prepare cases for the barristers who pleaded in the Common Law Courts. Chadwick decided to become a barrister. This meant starting again and another seven years before he could be called to the Bar. But his father agreed, and in 1823 he began at Lyons Inn in the Middle Temple.

While he worked in Lyons Inn as a law student Chadwick helped to keep himself by reporting for the newspapers. It was his newspaper work which first took him into the London slums and showed him their horrors. Also at this time he met two doctors who were to become friends for life—Neil Arnott and Southwood Smith. They sharpened his interest in medicine and hospitals, and with them he visited many of the worst fever spots in the East End.

The Influence of Jeremy Bentham
Chadwick's burning ambition now became social reform. He soon joined the circle of reformers who were working in London with Jeremy Bentham as their leader. In 1828 Chadwick made a hit with a long article on the condition of the London poor in the 'Westminster Review'. In 1829 he followed this up with an article in the London Review on 'Preventive Police'. People who were keen on reform approved of what he wrote and introduced him to Jeremy Bentham himself.

Bentham took to Chadwick and within a few weeks hired him as his secretary. They became firm friends, and in 1831 Chadwick left Lyons Inn and went to live at Bentham's home in Queens Square. He was with Bentham to the last, nursing him through his final illness, and was at his bedside when he died in April 1832.

This close friendship with Bentham was probably the 3

Jeremy Bentham

deepest influence of Chadwick's life. It altered the whole way
he looked at social reform. First Bentham taught Chadwick to
see problems logically, and not to be too impressed by how things
had been done in the past. Bentham's first question of any law
was 'what use is it?' We can see the way his mind worked in
what he said about the Game Laws which punished people for
killing birds or animals that rich men wanted to hunt for sport:
'I sow corn: partridges eat it, and if I attempt to defend it
against the partridges I am fined or sent to gaol: all this, for
fear a great man, who is above sowing corn, should be in want of
partridges.' This approach had a profound effect on Chadwick.
When he came to study the problem of the poor laws and
public health his solutions swept away the muddle of centuries.
Inevitably, this made the plans difficult to work because the
4   people who made a good thing out of the muddle opposed him.

Bentham's second influence was on Chadwick's idea of what the Government ought to do. Many people at this time believed that the Government should interfere as little as possible in the affairs of its citizens. In particular they believed that it was best if people were left free to get on with their business with as few restrictions as possible. This approach is usually called *'laissez-faire'* (letting things alone). Chadwick also believed in this general rule but through Bentham's teaching he came to see that sometimes the freedom of one group to do as it liked, harmed a lot of other people and the nation suffered. For instance, if builders were free to put up houses as cheaply as they liked with no water or drains and not enough ventilation, this harmed the people who had to live in them. They got sick and died early; and the country suffered from the waste of their manpower. Chadwick came to believe that in cases like this the Government should intervene. It took some time for this idea of the role of the Government to be accepted, and Chadwick's work, particularly on public health, played an important part in this process.

In 1832, as Bentham lay dying, Chadwick had both a strong ambition for social reform and a clear idea how to set about it. Just at this moment he was invited to join a Government enquiry into the Poor Laws. This was a turning point in his life. He gave up the Law, and was to devote the rest of his life to the public service.

2 The Old Poor Law

The state of the poor had been worrying the government for some time. The cost of looking after them had been rising dramatically, from £1,500,000 in 1775 to about £7,000,000 in 1832, and the poor themselves were growing more and more discontented. In 1830 there were serious riots by country labourers in the South; ricks were burned and machines were

Labourers burning a farm in Kent in 1830.

destroyed. The Government put down this 'labourers' revolt,' hanging nine people and *deporting* hundreds more. Clearly, something more permanent had to be done.

The Poor Law Commission

In February 1832 the Government announced that there would be a 'Royal Commission for Enquiring into the administration and practical operation of the Poor Laws.' The Royal Commission had eight distinguished members, including the Bishops of London and Chester, and Chadwick's friend Nassau Senior. At this stage Chadwick himself was not a member, but Nassau Senior asked him to be one of the Assistant Commissioners. His job was to find out how the Poor Laws worked in North and East London. It was not long, however, before he was also studying Berkshire, which was a very poor rural county.

After ten months work the group of Assistant Commissioners had gathered a mass of information, but the Commission was nowhere near being able to report. The Government and the public were becoming restive. So the Government asked each Assistant Commissioner to send in a selection from his evidence, and this was to be published immediately, in order to prepare public opinion for the changes which would be suggested in the full Report. Chadwick's evidence was a complete report in itself. It took up one third of the volume, and ended with several clear, practical, suggestions. The members of the Commission were most impressed, and asked the Lord Chancellor to appoint him a full Commissioner, so that he could help to draw up the final report. His name was added to the Commission, and in fact the Report which was published in February 1834 was written by Chadwick and Nassau Senior together.

First, the 1834 Report described how the existing Poor Laws worked. It was a very confusing and unsatisfactory situation. There was no one system in the country. Each parish, and there were 15,000 of them, looked after its own poor out of the *poor rates*, which were paid by householders. The old and sick were usually given money or food and some medical attention in their own homes. Those were not a problem, and the Report found that 'allowances to the aged and infirm are moderate,' and that 'medical attendance seems in general to be adequately supplied, and economically.'

The major problem was the relief which was given to the able-bodied poor. These were labourers who were fit enough to

7

Providing for and employing all the Poor in Gr. Britain

View of an eighteenth century workhouse with the paupers busy at various jobs – from a playing card

work but who for one reason or another did not earn enough money to keep themselves and their families. Here, the Report found a chaotic state of affairs, and the reason why the poor rates cost the country so much. In the year ending 25th March 1832 over £7 million was spent on the poor. This was one fifth of the entire national expenditure.

The able-bodied poor were given relief in several different ways. Those who had no job were usually paid money or given food. Sometimes the parish paid local farmers to employ those who applied for relief (this was called the roundsman system); sometimes the parish itself employed them, and sometimes a system called the labour-rate was used, by which the ratepayers (usually farmers) agreed to employ a number of labourers, not because they needed them, but in proportion to the amount of poor rates which they paid.

The Speenhamland System

Under the commonest system, particularly in the agricultural areas of the South, the able-bodied poor were paid an allowance to make up their low wages to an agreed minimum. This is often called the Speenhamland system. It was named after the Berkshire magistrates who met at Speenhamland in 1795 to decide what to do about wages for the agricultural labourers, since food prices were rising very quickly at that time. There were two plans before the magistrates. Either they could insist on a minimum wage for labourers, or they could make up the labourers' wages, so that they were enough to live on. The magistrates rejected the first plan, and agreed to make up wages according to a scale which rose with the price of bread and the number of children a labourer had.

Here is part of the table of weekly wages which the Speenhamland magistrates published.

"This shows us one part of what should be the Weekly Income of the Industrious Poor, as settled by the Magistrates for the county of Berks. at a Meeting held at Speenhamland, May the 6th, 1795.			Income should be for a Man	For a Single Woman	For a Man and his Wife	With One Child	With Two Children
When the gallon loaf is	1s	0d	3s 0d	2s 0d	4s 6d	6s 0d	7s 6d
When	,,	,,	1s 1d	3s 3d	2s 1d	4s 10d	6s 5d	8s 0d
When	,,	,,	1s 2d	3s 6d	2s 2d	5s 2d	6s 10d	8s 6d
When	,,	,,	1s 3d	3s 9d	2s 3d	5s 6d	7s 3d	9s 0d
When	,,	,,	1s 4d	4s 0d	2s 4d	5s 10d	7s 8d	9s 6d
When	,,	,,	1s 5d	4s 0d	2s 5d	5s 11d	7s 10d	9s 9d
When	,,	,,	1s 6d	4s 3d	2s 6d	6s 3d	8s 3d	10s 3d
When	,,	,,	1s 7d	4s 3d	2s 7d	6s 4d	8s 5d	10s 6d
When	,,	,,	1s 8d	4s 6d	2s 8d	6s 8d	8s 10d	11s 0d
When	,,	,,	1s 9d	4s 6d	2s 9d	6s 9d	9s 0d	11s 3d
When	,,	,,	1s 10d	4s 9d	2s 10d	7s 1d	9s 5d	11s 9d

Notice that when the gallon loaf of bread cost 1/-, a married man with two children was entitled to 7/6 a week. If his income only came to 6/-, he would have an extra 1/6 from the parish. As the price of bread rose, or as the family grew, so his weekly income would rise, whatever work he did or whatever his employer paid him.

This system spread very quickly through the agricultural areas of the South while food prices continued to rise because of the war with France. The Royal Commission also found that it was spreading in the North of England, though we now know that it was not very common there.

The Effect on Labourers

The spread of the allowance system kept labourers reasonably quiet at a time of high prices and low wages, but by 1834 it was becoming obvious that the system had very unfortunate effects in the long run. In particular, the Commission found that it had a bad effect on the labourers. It encouraged idleness, since there seemed no point in working if you could get the same amount of money without working or by working for the parish, which was often very nearly the same thing. It also took away much of the pride which good labourers had taken in their work, since they were made to feel fools for working hard when others got the same money for doing very little. Here is how Thomas Pearce, a Sussex labourer, described the situation, when he was interviewed.

'In your parish are there many able-bodied men upon the parish?'

'There are a great many men in our parish who like it better than being at work.'

'Why do they like it better?'

'They get the same money and don't do half so much work. They don't work like me; they be'ant at it so many hours, and they don't do so much work when they be at it; they're doing no good, and are only waiting for dinner-time and night; they be'ant working, it's only waiting.'

'How have you managed to live without parish relief?'

'By working hard.'

'What do the paupers say to you?

'They blame me for what I do. They say to me, "what are you working for?" I say "For myself" They say "You are only doing it to save the parish, and if you didn't do it, you would get the same as another man has, and would get the

Two views of an agricultural labourers life at home: (above) a late eighteenth century painting (below) a photograph taken around 1860. How do they differ?

money for smoking your pipe and doing nothing." Tis a hard thing for a man like me.'

Labourers under the allowance system were often idle, and, even worse, they did not care much about the future. They were discouraged from saving and trying to buy themselves a little land or a pig because if it became known that they had put something by they would not be allowed relief when they were unemployed. Labourers were also encouraged to marry and have a lot of children, because a man with a big family would always get a fair wage according to the scales. On one occasion Mr. Villiers, one of the Assistant Commissioners, went out to test this theory by asking the first labourers he met about it.

'The opportunity soon occurred; four men were working together near a farmhouse; upon questioning them as to the wages each was earning, one among them, who informed us that he was 30 years of age and unmarried, complained much of the lowness of his wages and added, without a question on the subject being put to him "That if he was a married man, and had a parcel of children, he should be better off, as he should either have work given him by the piece or receive allowances for his children. He was immediately joined by two of the other men who said: "Yes, Sir, that is how it is; a man has no chance now unless he is a family man."

You can well imagine that if a man married simply to get a better allowance or more work it was not likely to be a particularly happy marriage, and children who were born simply to raise the allowance would probably not be well looked after.

The Effect on Wages
Another important result of the system was that it kept wages low. Obviously farmers felt no need to increase wages when they knew that a labourer's low wages would be 'made up' out of the poor rates. Of course, farmers and others employers also paid the poor rates, but if you employed a number of men you saved more on their wages than you paid out in poor rates. Not all employers kept wages down like this, but it was quite

common. Also, in areas where the roundsman system was used, the farmers could always get paupers from the parish, and their wages were paid entirely out of the poor rates.

The Commission was worried not only because the poor rates were high, and the allowance system had a bad effect on the labourers, but also because of the effect which this in turn had on the country's wealth. They believed that the country could only get richer if labourers were honest and hard-working. So, clearly, if the Poor Laws were making the labourers idle and dishonest this would eventually make everybody poorer.

Those Who Did Well Out of the Old Poor Law

If the effects of the Poor Laws were so bad, why had they not been changed before this? Partly it was because nobody knew what to put in their place. Some people wanted all poor relief abolished, but most people feared that then there would be even worse riots and burnings than there had already been when times were bad. But also a lot of people did well out of the Poor Laws, though this only made them more costly and inefficient. Many labourers, particularly the idle ones, liked the allowance system. Many farmers, as we have seen, found that they could save more on wages than they paid in poor rates. There were also the many people who helped to spend the £7 million of poor rates.

We have seen that each parish was responsible for its own poor. So the parish vestry had to collect the poor rates and appoint an *overseer* for the poor. The vestry was a committee composed either of all the ratepayers who chose to attend, or a group elected by all the ratepayers. Usually the most regular attenders were those who had something to gain, often farmers or shopkeepers. Here is how the Report describes some of the temptations for the vestryman:

'If he is the owner of cottages, he endeavours to get their rent paid by the parish; if he keeps a shop, he struggles to get allowance for his customers or debtors; if he deals in articles used in the workhouse, he tries to increase the workhouse consumption.'
The Report concluded that vestries were 'the most irresponsible

bodies that ever were entrusted with the performance of public duties or the distribution of public money.'

The overseer was the man appointed by the vestry to collect the poor rate and dole out relief to those whom he thought needed it. The job was unpaid, and usually lasted a year, though sometimes only for six or three months. If the man was dishonest, the opportunities for fraud or favouritism were almost unlimited. Even when the overseer was honest it was almost impossible for him to be efficient. Usually he could not afford to spend much time on this unpaid work, and because he only did the job for a short time, he could not get enough knowledge or experience to be sure that he was giving relief to those who really needed it. In the few cases where a parish had a permanent, paid overseer, this was found to be much more efficient.

The Commission's Recommendations
The Commission's Report was not in favour of the existing Poor Laws. It showed that the system was inefficient, enormously costly, and in the long run was very bad for the labouring classes. What did it suggest should be done about it? The *'Remedial Measures'* which form the last half of the Report were written by Chadwick himself, and the principles on which they are based were his own suggestions. They are very simple and extremely ingenious. When they were put into the Poor Law Amendment Act (1834) they produced what was probably the most hated single law of the nineteenth century.

First Chadwick wanted to restore the self-respect of the independent labourer which had been destroyed by the allowance system. He proposed to do this by making it less attractive to be a pauper than even the worst paid independent labourer.

Secondly, Chadwick wanted to develop a foolproof system to make sure that relief was only given to those who were really in need. His answer to this problem was the workhouse-test. Anyone who applied for relief would only be able to get it by going into the workhouse. If the workhouse was made sufficient-

ly unattractive, the very fact that someone was prepared to go into it would prove that he or she really needed help. In this way there would be no need for complicated rules to decide when someone should get relief; all *outdoor relief,* that is, all relief given to people who were still living outside the workhouse in their own homes, could be abolished, and the millions of pounds which were spent on people who were not really in need would be saved. This sounds very sensible but it meant one thing which would be a bitter blow to many: fathers, mothers and children would be separated and put in separate parts of the workhouse.

These were the two main changes which the Commission suggested. The rest of the 'Remedial Measures' suggest the arrangements for working the new ideas. First the Report proposed a Central Board of Poor Law Commissioners who would make sure that the law was properly carried out throughout the country, and not bent by local pressures. Next it proposed that numbers of parishes should be formed into groups to be known as Unions, because individual parishes could not afford the separate workhouses for the young, the sick, and the able-bodied men and women which the Report recommended. The Unions would be run by Boards of Guardians, elected· by the ratepayers, who would be responsible for working the Poor Law in their Unions. The Board of Guardians would in turn be responsible to the Central Poor Law Commissioners. The Guardians would have to appoint permanent paid overseers, workhouse masters, medical officers, etc. This scheme with its central control and staff of full-time paid employees was in itself a revolutionary suggestion, and many people complained bitterly about the spread of '*bureaucracy*' and 'centralisation', but it is in fact the basis of our system of local government today.

3 The Poor Law Amendment Act

The Royal Commission's Report, published in February 1834, was an instant success. 10,000 copies were given away to influence public opinion, and a further 10,000 copies were bought. The Government of the day, which represented, by and large, the great landed families who were most worried by

A cartoon published in 1836

the cost of the poor rates, accepted the conclusions of the Report. The Poor Law Amendment Act which they passed in 1834 followed its main recommendations.

But there were important differences between the Report and the Act, which made difficulties when the Law was put into operation. The Report had recommended that 'all relief whatever to able-bodied persons or their families, otherwise than in well regulated workhouses shall be declared unlawful, and shall cease.' The Act only said that the Central Board should 'regulate outdoor relief.' This lead to serious differences of opinion on how the Law should operate, but it was a sensible move. The complete abolition of outdoor relief would have been impossibly severe.

More important were the differences in the powers of the Central Board. The Report had intended the Central Board to have the power to compel local Boards of Guardians to raise the necessary poor rates in order to build proper workhouses, and to be able to imprison for contempt of court those who refused. These powers were very much reduced in the Act. The Board had no power to imprison anyone, and could only levy a compulsory rate up to £50 or one tenth of the annual rate. As a result, the Central Board did not really have enough power to make the Guardians take action, though it was usually able to prevent them from doing things it disapproved of. Because of this many of the reforms which Chadwick would have liked to see, such as district schools, better sanitation, and separate workhouses for the old and sick, children and adults, never happened.

The Poor Law Commissioners
The Poor Law Amendment Act set up a Central Board of three Poor Law *Commissioners*. Chadwick had been sure that he, as the main author of the plan, would be appointed one of the Commissioners. Nowadays, it is very likely that he would have been, but in 1834 these Commissionerships, with their salary of £2,000 p.a. were thought of as 'jobs,' that is rewards, to people who had supported either the Whig or Tory Parties. In fact, only one of the Commissioners, George Nicholls, had any 17

practical experience of the Poor Laws. Shaw Lefevre, whom Chadwick described as 'about as fit to act for the Poor Law Amendment Act as a delicate girl would be to assist in performing an amputation,' was a friend of the Whig Government. The other Commissioner was a country gentleman called Frankland Lewis who was appointed to keep the Tory opposition happy. Chadwick was passed over—'it was considered that his station in society was not as would have made it fit that he should be made one of the Commissioners.' He was, however, very reluctantly, and only by appealing to his sense of public duty, persuaded to accept the job as secretary. It was suggested that he would be treated more like a fourth Commissioner, and should be next in line for promotion.

So the Poor Law Board with Chadwick as its Secretary set to work to put in hand the New Poor Law. Assistant Commissioners were appointed to supervise the grouping of parishes

Thomas Frankland Lewis

into Unions and the election of Boards of Guardians. The Central Board sent out orders about the way workhouses were to be planned and the kind of food they were to give the paupers in them. When a Union had been formed, and a suitable workhouse provided, a general order was sent to that Union stopping outdoor relief to the able-bodied poor, and making them apply to the workhouse. But it was slow work. When the Board had completed a survey of the number of workhouses already available they were found to be far too few, and 350 new ones had to be built in the first five years.

The job was not made any easier by the continual quarrelling and battling between members of the Central Board. Chadwick and Frankland Lewis took an immediate dislike for each other and this made their differences of opinion all the more bitter. Chadwick maintained that the Act should be applied as quickly as possible, while the good harvests and healthy state of trade during 1834-6 lasted. In particular he thought that the Act should be applied to the North as soon as possible, because he knew that it would create fierce opposition there. But the Commissioners began by extending the working of the Act slowly in the South. In 1837 they began to enforce it in the North, and at the same time harvests were bad, trade declined, and the country started on one of the severest depressions of the century.

Opposition in the North
The result was bitter and violent opposition. The allowance system had never been common in the north, and the workers needed public relief in times of depression, when there was no work to do. Also, they hated the idea of workhouses, with their discipline, poor food and separation of families. The factory workers were already quite well organised and they were stirred up by radical leaders, like Richard Oastler and the Rev. Joseph Stephens. Here is an extract from a famous sermon preached by Stephens, which will give an idea of the wild passion with which the New Poor Law was opposed in the North.

'The people are not going to stand this. I will say that sooner than wife and husband and father and son shall be 19

The attack on the workhouse at Stockport in 1842. The rioters are handing out bread

sundered and dungeoned and fed on *'skillee'*—sooner than wife and daughter shall wear the prison dress—sooner than that—Newcastle ought to be, and shall be one blaze of fire with only one way to put it out, and that with the blood of all who support this abominable measure.'

In some places there were riots, Assistant Commissioners were attacked, and Boards of Guardians were driven out of town. We can get a good idea of what it was like when this happened from the report which Assistant Commissioner A. Power sent to the Board about the events at Bradford when he tried to apply the Act there.

The first meeting of the Bradford Board of Guardians, attended by Mr. Power on 30th October 1837, had to be abandoned when the crowd forced the door of the courthouse. The Guardians retired to the Sun Hotel. Here one of the local magistrates said that the crowd wanted to know what was going on, and that the Board should hold an open meeting at the courthouse. This they agreed to do, and met the public at 2.00 p.m. 'Nothing could exceed the confusion which prevailed during the meeting, and the greatest possible *exasperation* was evinced against the Law.' Nevertheless, 'amidst great noise and confusion' various administrative recommendations were adopted. Then Mr. Power continues: 'On leaving the courthouse I was violently assaulted. The first blow I received was upon my head from a tin can. Umbrellas, stones and mud were applied very freely, and after receiving many blows I *extricated* myself with great difficulty . . . and reached the Inn by dint of great exertion, being pushed almost to the door.'

Mr. Power asked the Central Board for six metropolitan policemen to protect the next meeting on November 13th. These were sent and arrived on November 4th, but the townspeople got to hear of their arrival. The meeting on November 13th was postponed for fear of a serious riot, and a troop of cavalry was sent for, to settle in before the meeting on November 30th and frighten the crowd. Mr. Power in fact decided not to attend that meeting, and the day's events were reported to him by the Clerk of the Union, Mr. Wagstaff. The Board met at 11.00 a.m. and set to work.

'During this time the mob kept *aloof*, but, a party of them having found their way through the special constables to the door of the courthouse, both the military and the building were immediately assaulted with stones; and at this time (about 12.00) Mr. Paley, the magistrate, read the Riot Act.

'From this time until the close of the meeting the cavalry appear to have vainly attempted the *dispersion* of the crowd, acting with the greatest possible *forbearance*, and using their *sabres* only, so far as I can learn.

'The magistrates and Guardians appear to have left the courthouse without any serious *molestation;* but Mr. Wagstaff, the Clerk was detained in the building and beset by the mob for some hours . . . About five o'clock Mr. Wagstaff was rescued from his perilous situation by a detachment of the Cavalry. On returning through the

Reading the Riot Act

streets to the Talbot Inn the crowd closed upon the party in such a manner as to make it necessary to charge them, when several shots were fired, and some persons cut down.

'Many persons have been seriously hurt, both by sabre and gunshot wounds, but it does not appear that any death has yet occurred.'

Chadwick's Position at the Board

While the Assistant Commissioners were struggling to introduce the New Poor Law in the country, Chadwick's position at the Central Board grew worse. Frankland Lewis resigned in December 1838, and when the new Commissioner was appointed it was not Chadwick but Frankland Lewis's son George Cornewall Lewis. After this, Chadwick could hardly persuade the Commissioners to do anything he wanted. The pity of this is that Chadwick, unlike Lewis, was interested in preventing poverty, not just in keeping down the rates.

22

For this reason Chadwick encouraged James Kay, an Assistant Commissioner, to study the education of pauper children. He realised that orphans, for instance, must be given an education which would fit them for a job when they left the workhouse. Otherwise they would never be able to earn their own living, and so would continue to be paupers and a burden on the rates. Kay's report showed the need to set up district schools, where poor children could be properly taught, away from the bad influence of the grown-up paupers in the workhouse. Such schools would bring together children from a number of Unions, would be able to afford proper schoolteachers, and would prepare poor children for a useful life. Here is an example of the sort of daily programme which would be followed in one of these schools.

6.00	rise, wash, dress.
6.20	rollcall, inspection.
6.30	prayers, breakfast.
7.15–8.00	recreation in yards.
8.00–11.00	boys–gardening or carpentering, shoe making, whitewashing etc.
	girls–make beds, scrub floors, work in laundry, kitchen.
11.00–12.00	reading from bible, hymn singing.
12.00	lunch.
12.30–2.00	recreation in yards.
2.00–4.00	reading in lesson books, writing, arithmetic, etc.
4.00–5.00	religious instruction.
5.00–6.00	singing.
6.00	supper. After supper, prayers, hymns and bed.

This doesn't sound much fun, but it would have been better for the children than being left with all the older folk in the workhouses. However, the Poor Law Commissioners had very little time for this sort of thing. Although they had the power after 1844, only about ten district schools were ever built.

Another cause of poverty which began to interest Chadwick was dirt and disease. As he could no longer get his plans for the

Poor Law carried out, he began to study and think about the problem of public health. This, as we shall see in later chapters, became his life's work, and his most important contribution to history.

A workhouse yard in the 1840s. Notice that the women have a separate yard from the men and are all wearing the same workhouse dress.

4 The New Poor Law in Action – Stow Union in Suffolk

So far we have been looking at the old Poor Laws and the Poor Law Amendment Act as they affected the nation as a whole. But if we want to understand how the New Poor Law really worked and how it affected people's lives, we need to look at a detailed example. Fortunately, we can still learn how the New Poor Law was applied, because many of the records of the Unions which were formed under it have survived, and you can study them in most County Record Offices.

The account which follows is of one Union—Stow Union in Suffolk. Suffolk is a good county to look at because in 1834 it was almost entirely agricultural, and the cost of poor relief there was one of the highest in the country. This was just the sort of area which the New Poor Law was meant to deal with. Stow Union is a good one to study because many of its records have survived. But beware of thinking that what happened at Stow necessarily happened throughout the country. This may not be so. If you remember this, however, a close look at Stow Union can give a clearer picture of the New Poor Law in action.

Stow Union

Stow Union was formed in March 1835 by Assistant Commissioner Mott. As you can see from the map it consisted of 34 parishes and was divided into three main districts—Stowmarket, Walsham-le-Willows, and Rattlesden. The fourteen parishes round Stowmarket itself had been formed into Stow Hundred in 1781. This probably made the formation of Stow Union fairly easy, since parishes in that area were already used to doing everything together rather than running their own affairs. Notice that Stowmarket makes a natural centre for this Union. It was then a small market town midway between the

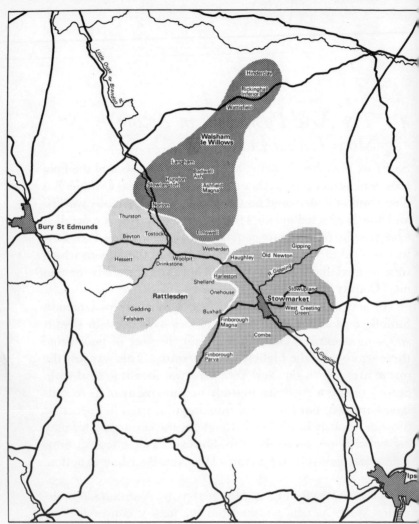

Map of Stow Union

larger county towns of Ipswich and Bury St. Edmunds.

After forming the Union, the first task was to elect a Board of Guardians, who would run the Poor Law business in Stow Union. The Guardians were elected by the ratepayers, and were unpaid. In this case, each of the thirty-four parishes elected one Guardian, except Stowmarket which elected two. In addition, there were seven people who became Guardians because of the

26

position they held—J.Ps., and the more important clergymen. The Stow Union Board of Guardians had a total of forty-two members, but at the weekly Board meetings fewer than half used to attend, and sometimes there are only six people listed in the minutes.

Although the Board of Guardians was responsible for running Stow Union, most of the work was done by full-time paid employees. This was a great change from the old Poor Law system of unpaid part-time overseers of the poor who only did the job for a short period. The officers appointed under the New Poor Law became professional paid local government officials. They helped to create a local government system as we know it. We can tell from the accounts of Stow Union who these officials were and what they were paid. First there was a secretary to the Board, who kept the minutes of meetings and the accounts, and who did all the Board's correspondence. He was paid £100 a year. Then there were three Relieving Officers, one for each district of the Union, at salaries of £90 per year. These were the people to whom the poor applied for relief when they were in distress. There were also three 'surgeons' or doctors as we would now call them. Again there was one for each district and their salaries varied according to the number of people in each district £133, £112, and £108 a year. They were the best paid Poor Law Officials in this Union. Then there was a Governor of the Workhouse, at £80 a year, and his wife who was matron at £20. They also got free lodging in the workhouse and presumably free food. Also at the workhouse there was a schoolmaster and his wife who were paid £30 a year. We can guess that at that salary they were probably not much good, and the minutes often refer to schoolmasters resigning or being dismissed. There were probably other people employed at the workhouse, such as a nurse, but we do not know how much they were paid. Finally there was a chaplain to the Union, who was paid £50 a year.

The Workhouse

In many cases when a Union was formed there was no adequate workhouse, so that the Union had to build one before it could begin to apply the workhouse test. Stow Union was fortunate because it already had a large handsome workhouse. This is how it is described in White's Directory of Suffolk (1844):

'The Union Workhouse, standing on an *eminence* in the parish of Onehouse, more than half a mile West of Stowmarket, was erected in 1781 as a House of Industry for the 14 parishes of Stow Hundred, which were incorporated under Gilberts Act. It cost more than £12,000 and was described in 1810 as having more the appearance of a gentlemen's *seat* than a receptacle for paupers.' The building still stands today, and is now Stow Lodge Hospital. As you can see from this photograph, it is a very fine building. The small brick building at the entrance is new and there were probably no rose bushes in front in 1835, but otherwise the outside of the building is just as it was then. It looks much more attractive than many of the workhouses which were built in other parts of the country.

Fortunately, the actual plans for this building have been preserved, so that we can tell in detail how it was arranged inside. Here are the plans for the ground floor, Chamber (first floor), and Attick Story (second floor). Notice that the workhouse was very much self-supporting, with cows, pigs, a mill house, bakery, and brew house. Also notice the worksheds, the cells for lunatics and the small rooms for married couples. When

Stow Workhouse at it is today—a hospital

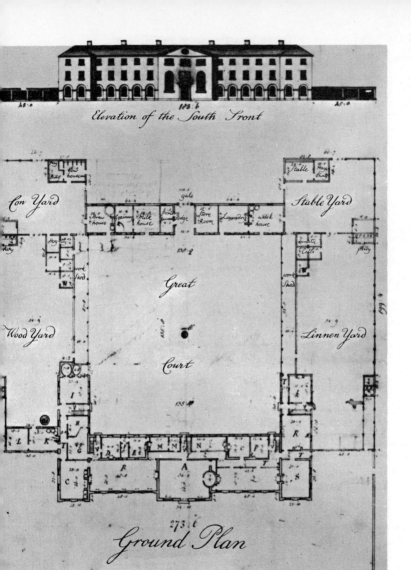

Elevation of the South Front

Ground Plan

original plans for Stow Workhouse (see also overleaf)

REFERENCES TO GROUND PLAN

Chapel	G Pantry	N School Room	T Passages
Dining Room	H Bread Room	O Spare Room	V Staircase
Kitchen	I Bake Room	P Overseer's Room	k Infirmary
Governor's Room	K Scullery	Q Work Room	W Coal Bins
Governor's Parlour	L Dairy	R Work Room	
Governor's Pantry	M Apothecary's Room	S Store Room	

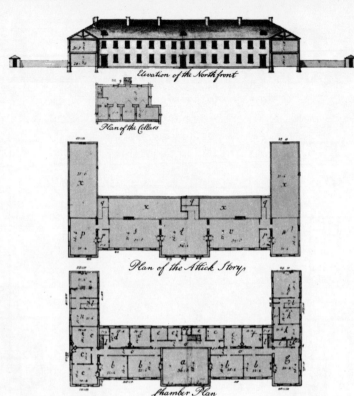

Elevation of the North front

Plan of the Cellars

Plan of the Attick Story

Chamber Plan

REFERENCES TO THE CHAMBER STORY

a Chapel continued
b Bed Rooms
c Governor's Bed Rooms
d Bed Rooms
e Bed Rooms for
  married people
f Bed Room
g Committee Room
h Closet for wrightings

i Closet
k Infirmary
l Staircases
m Cheese and
  flower Room
n Bed room for Baker
o Passages
p Bed Room for Girls
q Staircases

REFERENCES TO THE ATTICK STORY

r Bed Rooms
s Bed Rooms
t Bed Room
v Bed Room
w Bed Rooms for Boys
x In Roofs

the workhouse was taken over by Stow Union the internal arrangement was altered to bring it into line with the Commissioner's rules about workhouses. We do not have the plans for these alterations but we do have plans which were published as examples by the Poor Law Commissioners. Here is one for a workhouse of about 200, a little smaller than Stow workhouse. We can guess that the small bedrooms in the old Stow workhouse were knocked into larger dormitories, where the

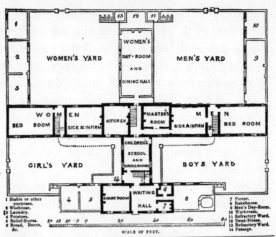

Plans for a workhouse of 200 published by the Poor Law Commissioners

1 Stable or other purposes.
2 Washhouse.
3 Laundry.
4 Potatoes.
5 Relief-Stores.
6 Bread, Bacon, &c.
7 Porter.
8 Bakehouse.
9 Men's Day-Room.
10 Workroom.
11 Refractory Ward.
12 Dead-House.
13 Refractory Ward.
14 Passage.

SCALE OF FEET.

[K.] No. 2. One Pair Plan.

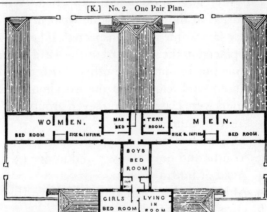

31

men and women were separated from each other and from the boys and girls. There would also have been separate rooms for the aged and infirm. The little rooms for married people would almost certainly have disappeared. The new workhouse also had its *refractory wards,* which do not appear on the earlier plans. These were small cells, often without windows, into which paupers were put if they misbehaved. Perhaps they used the old 'lunatic cells.' The yard was also probably divided to provide separate exercise yards for the different classes of pauper.

No rule book for Stow workhouse has survived, but it must have followed the Poor Law Commissioners' very detailed 'orders and regulations to be observed in the workhouse'. We can therefore guess what happened. When a pauper was admitted to the workhouse he went first to a *probationary ward* where he was medically inspected. If he was sick or an idiot, he was placed in the sick ward or the ward for lunatics. Otherwise he was put in one of the other wards after being 'thoroughly cleansed' and 'clothed in the workhouse dress.' Officially the paupers were classified into seven groups.

1. Aged or infirm.
2. Able-bodied men and youths above 13.
3. Youths and boys above 7 and under 13.
4. Aged or infirm women.
5. Able-bodied women and girls above 16.
6. Girls above 7 and under 16.
7. Children under 7.

But this grouping was too elaborate for many workhouses. Each group had to have separate rooms where they were to remain 'without communication,' except that mothers were to be allowed to see their children under seven 'at all reasonable times.' The rule could be relaxed for married couples who were aged or infirm, when there were 'special reasons' which were approved by the Poor Law Commissioners. The separation of families (done for 'moral' reasons) and the workhouse dress, were the two things which the poor hated most bitterly.

Each day the paupers would rise early and assemble for
32   prayers and rollcall. After this came breakfast which, like all

meals, was eaten in silence. During the day the men were put to work often on hated tasks like oakum picking and bone crushing. Oakum picking meant untwisting lengths of old rope and picking the fibres apart. The fibres were then sold and spun again for use in ropes or cheap mats. The women were employed in 'household work.' Children were supposed to have at least three hours schooling 'in reading. writing, and in the principles of the Christian religion; and such other instructions shall be imparted to them as are calculated to train them to habits of usefulness, industry and virtue'. At Stow workhouse we know that the boys were taught gardening because a minute of 8th August 1837, records: 'ordered that the half acre of land used as a drying ground be appropriated to the purpose of horticulture by the boys in the workhouse under the superintendence of the schoolmaster and a committee.' There were more prayers after supper, and the day ended early, at 9 p.m. when the Master and Matron had to visit the wards and make sure that 'all fires and lights are extinguished.'

Any pauper could 'quit the workhouse, upon giving the Master three hours notice of his wish to do so'. But when extreme distress had forced you into the workhouse you were not likely to be able to take advantage of this unless you were lucky enough to find a job. Also a man with a family could only leave if he took his whole family with him. Finally, no-one could visit a pauper in the workhouse without permission from the Master, and even then the visit had to take place 'in the presence of the Master or Matron.'

The food which was given to paupers was very strictly regulated in an attempt to make the diet 'less eligible' (that is, more unpleasant) than the food which the lowest paid independent labourer ate. We can tell exactly what this food was for Stow workhouse since the approved diet sheet for 1838 has been preserved. Overleaf is a photograph of the poster which had to be displayed in the workhouse.

This diet looks grim, and indeed it probably was. Notice the monotony of it, and the fact that meat was only served once a week. We should remember, however, that if the food was fresh (sometimes it was not) and was supplied in full, this diet

STOW UNION

DIETARY

FOR ABLE-BODIED MEN AND WOMEN.

		BREAKFAST.	DINNER.					SUPPER.	
		Bread.	Gruel.	Meat pudding with Vegetables.	Suet pudding with Vegetables.	Bread.	Cheese.	Broth.	Bread.	Cheese.
		oz.	Pints.	oz.	oz.	oz.	oz.	Pints.	oz.	oz.
SUNDAY	Men	6 7	1½			7 8	1		6 7	1
	Women	5	1½			7	1		5	1
MONDAY	Men	6 7	1½	16					6 7	1
	Women	5	1¼	19					5	1
TUESDAY	Men	6 7	1½			7 8	1	½	6 7	1
	Women	5	1½			7	1	½	5	1
WEDNESDAY,	Men	6 7	1½		16				6 7	1
	Women	5	1½		19/12				5	1
THURSDAY	Men	6 7	1½			7 8	1		6 7	1
	Women	5	1½			7	1		5	1
FRIDAY	Men	6 7	1½		16				6 7	1
	Women	5	1½		19/12				5	1
SATURDAY	Men	6 7	1½			7 8		1½	6 7	1
	Women	5	1½			7		1¼	5	1

Old People, of Sixty Years of Age, and upwards, to be allowed 1 oz. of Tea, 5 oz. of Butter, and 7 oz. of Sugar per Week, in lieu of Gruel, for Breakfast.

Children under nine Years to be dieted at discretion; above Nine years to be allowed the same quantities as Women.

Sick to be dieted as directed by the Medical Officer.

Diet sheet for Stow Union

was probably better than the worst paid independent labourers lived on, in spite of the fact that it was supposed to be worse.

Life in the workhouse must have been very bleak and hard. But many workhouses probably were not as bad as people said they were. Much of history is the record of things which people remember and what people remember about the workhouses are the scandals—dreadful stories about paupers fighting to gnaw the bones they were supposed to be crushing, and brutal masters flogging and assaulting the paupers. We know that these things happened, but they were not common. They were news because they were rare. Stow Union workhouse does not seem to have been involved in any great scandals. It was

Two views of a workhouse meal: (above) a sketch published in 1840 (below) a photograph taken in a large London workhouse later in the century. Do you think the artist's sketch is likely to be accurate?

probably a better-than-average workhouse to be in. It certainly does not appear to have had any great problems over discipline. We know this because the workhouse Punishment Book from 1856–1878 has survived and we can see how many people were punished and for what offences. In the first four years from 1856 there were 27, 20, 13, and 22 people punished. This is quite a small number each year in a workhouse of over 200. Here is a selection of offences and their punishments recorded in the book.

Name	Offence	Date	Punishment
Mary Still	*Clandestinely* leaving her day ward and stealing 4 oz. of bread from the dining room.	6th Jan. 1856	8 oz. of bread for dinner 2 days.
George Spink Obadiah Spink	Damaging oakum by wetting it.	11th Feb. 1856	2 days in the refractory ward— bread and water.
John Wetherall Joseph Watts Edward Palmer	General inattention during schools.	29th Jan. 1857	6 stripes with the cane.
Robert Fuller	Dead drunk	2nd Aug. 1857.	Bread and water 2 days.
James Rudland	Smoking in bed in aged men's sleeping ward.	1st Mar. 1862.	Tea stopped for 7 days.

We can learn quite a lot about the workhouse from this list. People were punished for stealing food, which probably shows that their diets left them hungry. The offence of damaging oakum or refusing to work on it is common, because the men hated working on it so. Caning seems to have been reserved for the children. Adults were usually put on bread and water, and if they were particularly bad, put in the refractory ward. Nobody was allowed to drink alcohol in the workhouse, so that Robert Fuller probably got 'dead drunk' outside the workhouse, possibly whilst looking for a job. Probably the old men were not allowed to smoke in bed because of the fire risk but rules like this made life very bleak and lacking in comforts.

The workhouse was the centre of the Poor Law Business, but there were many other things for the Guardians and new officers to deal with. We can get an insight into the varied business of this Poor Law Union from the minutes of the weekly meeting of Guardians. Much of their time was taken up with routine work, assessing the Poor Rate which each parish had to pay, passing bills and paying salaries. Sometimes there would be complaints to investigate.

> '2nd May 1837. Mr. Freeman of Walsham also attended the Board and explained satisfactorily to them his reasons for not visiting Francis Finter on the evening he received the churchwardens' order, viz.—that he (Mr. Freeman) was engaged with a woman in case of labour with her first child: that from the enquiries he made, he found the pauper's case was not one of great urgency being a rheumatic affliction in the loins, and he attended the pauper as soon as his engagements permitted, the next morning and before he received any *intimation* that a complaint had been made to the Board.'

Sometimes there were special requests from paupers to consider. '8th November 1836. John Taylor of Rattlesden applied for a loan to assist him in migrating to Yarmouth for work, of £1 10s., a check was given to him accordingly and Rattlesden directed to be debited for the amount'. Finally, there was constant reference back to the Poor Law Commissioners in London, sometimes to answer their queries, sometimes for approval of actions of the Guardians, and sometimes, as in this case, for advice. '16th May 1837. Ordered that the clerk be directed to apply to the Poor Law Commissioners for instructions how the Board should act in the case of Balaam's family who having been sent by their Union into Yorkshire under contract to a manufacturer have broken their contract and become chargeable to the parish of Halifax, the overseer of which parish has applied for the amount of relief given them, under an implied threat of an order of removal.'

Outdoor Relief

Finally, the Guardians had the major job of controlling outdoor relief, i.e. relief given to paupers outside the workhouse. The original intention of the 1834 Report was to abolish all outdoor relief to able-bodied paupers. If a pauper really needed relief he should go into the workhouse. The purpose of the 'workhouse test' was, of course, to discourage the idlers who had been happy to live on 'allowances' without working.

Chadwick and the other Poor Law Commissioners quarrelled violently about how strictly this law was to be applied. Chadwick was for abolishing all outdoor relief completely, but the Commissioners wanted to go much more slowly. The law was never strictly enforced in the Northern towns where in the depression of 1838-41 the workhouses were full and labourers had to have outdoor relief or starve. But even in the agricultural areas like Suffolk we can see that Boards of Guardians used their own common sense as to how strict they could be.

In Stow Union outdoor relief was heavily reduced, but still more money was spent on it than on the people who lived in the workhouse. According to Whites Directory of Suffolk (1855) the 34 parishes of Stow Union spent on average £14,919 on poor relief in the three years before the Union was formed, but only £7,768 in 1838 and £7,754 in 1840. From the accounts which have survived we can compare the amount spent on outdoor relief by the 14 parishes of the old Stow Hundred. This table shows the amount spent by each parish in 1833 and 1840, together with its population in 1834 and 1841:

Parish	Outdoor relief 1833	1840	Population 1831	1841	Parish	Outdoor relief 1833	1840	Population 1831	1841
	£	£				£	£		
Buxhall	253	163	466	533	Stowmarket	813	439	2,672	3,043
Combs	338	229	950	1,064	Stow Upland	220	129	826	903
Creeting	115	81	166	213	Wetherden	284	208	487	515
Gt. Finborough	254	100	421	467					
Lt. Finborough	3	0	73	64	Totals	£3,177	£1,829	8,308	8,765
Gipping	140	71	87	93					
Harlston	67	35	89	90					
Hawleigh	232	121	908	916					
Old Newton	322	170	679	712					
Onehouse	84	60	358	43					
Shelland	52	23	126	109					

Although the total population had gone up by 457 the amount spent on outdoor relief had declined by £1,348. Nevertheless, £1,829 is still a substantial sum to be spent on outdoor relief after the New Poor Law had begun to work.

We can see what happened in more detail since some of the relief books have been preserved. There are two extracts on pages 40–41, both from the Parish of Stowmarket, one in 1830 and the second in 1845. We can notice certain obvious differences. The 1830 extract shows part of a page from a single week when a total of 82 people were relieved. In the 1845 extract each horizontal line marks a week, so we can see that only 4 to 8 people were relieved each week. Notice also that in 1830 each pauper was given money, and in quite substantial amounts when you remember that ten shillings a week was thought to be a good wage in those days. In 1845 less money and more food was given (called relief in kind). In 1845 those who got outdoor relief were on the whole elderly, and the younger ones were admitted to the workhouse. Usually the old were not considered to be 'able-bodied' so Boards of Guardians were allowed to give them relief in their own homes.

How the Act Worked in Stow Union

That is a brief account of how the New Poor Law was applied in Stow Union. How successful was it? We know that throughout the country the poor hated the new legislation and bitterly resented its workings. But how did it look to the governing classes—the people who had the job of applying it? We discover that in Stow Union they thoroughly approved of the new law, because in February 1837 the Guardians passed a resolution about it which was entered in the minutes. It is worth quoting in full since it gives a very different impression from most of the attacks on the New Poor Law which have been recorded since 1834:

'It was resolved *unanimously* that the Resolution now read to the Meeting be adopted and signed on behalf of the Board, and be inserted in the Bury and Ipswich papers.

'This Board views with regret the attempts that are continually made to bring the Poor Law Amendment Act into

The Overseer of *Newmarket* prays for Relief for the Underme...

PAUPERS' NAMES.	Quarterly Allowance.			By Weekly Committee.			Paid by Overseer.			When ordered.
Amt. bt. forward	£	s.	d.	8	13	9	£	s.	d.	
John Barnard					2	8				
Benjmn Barnard					3	0				
George Barnard					2	0				
John Barnard					2	0				
James Buxton					7	0				
Thomas Brett					5	6				
John Broom					4	6				
Valentine Barnard wf					1	0				
Willm Bailey					2	0				
Willm Baldwin					4	0				
John Buckle					2	6				

Mow UNION.

B.—FORM 10.   ABSTRACT of the APPLICATION and REPORT

Name of Applicant.	Age.	Particulars, and Number of Family.	Relief given, if at discretion of Reli...	
			Value in Kind.	
			s.	d.
Emerson Elizabeth	68			
Barnard William	64			
Barnard Henry	39	Wife & 5 Cn		
Ward Sarah	76			
Barnard William	64			
Chickens John	46	Wife & 6 Cn	1	
Ward Sarah	76		1	5
Thing Elizabeth	57			
Barnard Wm	64			
Ward Sarah	76		1	
Denny William	56	Wife & 4 Cn		
Hearn Ann	57	One Cn		

40   *Above: extract from the relief book of 1830. Below: extract from the relief book of 1845*

Cause of Complaint.	Belong to	Reside in	Remarks.
In distress	Stow mkt	Stow. n &c	
do	do	do	
do	do	do	
do	do	do	
do & a fist	do	do	
do	do	do	
do	do	do	
He in Prison	do		
In distress	do	do	
do	do	do	
do	do	do	

Parish of *Stowm...*

with Board's decisions on Applications for the Quarter ending *March* 1845

Relief ordered by Guardians.

Money.		Kind.			For what time allowed, or nature of the Order made
s.	d.	Quantity and Description.	s. Value. d.		
14					to St George with Wm Watkins
1		½ st		9	
					admitted
					M. & R.O.
1		½ Sif		9	
		do do	1		
6		Journey to Bil			M & R.O
					discover? being &c
1		½ st		9	
					M & R O
					admitted
1		½ st		9	

disrepute with the Public and to *stigmatise* as oppressors of the Poor those who are employed in carrying its provisions into effect.

'The Board have been now acting in the execution of the Bill more than twelve months and think themselves justified in pronouncing it sound in principle, producing practical results exceeding their expectations and requiring but little alteration in detail.

'The expenditure of the several parishes in this Union has been reduced in the *aggregate* $44\frac{3}{4}\%$ without diminishing the comforts of the aged and infirm. The Board attribute this reduction mainly to their having offered admission to the House instead of giving money out of doors to those whose idleness and *improvidence* formerly made them continuous applicants for Relief.

'That symptoms of returning industry are clearly visible amongst this class throughout the Union.

'That in particular this Board is convinced that the present arrangements for medical relief are such as to ensure attention to the wants of the Poor.

'That this Board is fully sensible of the *Utility* of the Poor Law Commissioners in producing a unity of operations throughout the country.

'That this address be signed by the Chairman on behalf of the meeting and be forwarded to His Majesty's Secretary of State for Home Affairs and that a copy of the same be sent to Dr. Kay the Assistant Poor Law Commissioner.'

This wholehearted approval should not surprise us when we remember that the Guardians represented the class who paid the poor rates and they were delighted that the rates were cheaper. In spite of the violent anti-Poor Law agitation, the Law remained in force for about 100 years.

What the Act Achieved
Nowadays our judgement on the Poor Law Amendment Act would be rather different. It was certainly effective in reducing the cost of poor relief. This was £7,870,801 in 1818, £7,036,968 in 1832 but only £4,044,741 in 1837. After that the cost rose

with the depression but settled around £5 million a year, in spite of the rising population. But the men who made the Act did not really understand the causes of poverty. The allowance system was singled out as the main cause, and the Act was planned to deal with it quite well. But the allowance system did not apply in the north. Here, the main causes of poverty were the periodic trade depressions which threw thousands out of work. At times like these, an Act to discourage the idler made no sense, since there was no work to be had however much he wanted it. Then temporary relief was essential to see him through until trade picked up again, and the Board did eventually recognise this. In the south the allowance system was one of the main causes of low wages and the depressing condition of the labourers. But it was not the only cause.

There were also too many labourers in the country districts and the settlement laws prevented them from moving. Under these laws a parish was responsible for looking after only the paupers who had a settlement there—since 1834 this meant those who were born there. If you fell ill or out of work in a parish where you did not have a settlement you could be forcibly removed to your parish of settlement. This obviously discouraged labourers from moving freely to places where there was more work.

This seems an odd law to us now but it comes down from the time of serfdom when peasants literally belonged on the land and were not allowed to move. Remember also that the cost of looking after its poor was borne by each parish through the poor rates, and no parish was prepared to look after someone else's paupers. Although the New Poor Law had taken away from the parishes the job of looking after the poor, it had not changed the settlement laws in the same way. Chadwick had wanted it to do this. In his thorough way he had noticed that most paupers were only removed short distances. In St. Pauls parish only 45 out of 840 removals were beyond 12 miles. He had proposed to make the Union the legal area for settlement so that it would be possible for paupers to move anywhere within the Union. This would almost certainly have cut down on the enormous amount of time and money which was 43 wasted on sending paupers back to their original parish. Nowadays we get round this problem because everybody contributes equally through taxes and national insurance. It does not matter where you fall ill or out of work, because it is not the local parish which has to pay for you.

Chadwick urged his view again in 1846 before a *select committee*, but when a new law was passed that year it only said that a person could not be removed if he had lived 5 years in a parish. It was another twenty years before the Union Chargeability Act (1865) prevented paupers being forcibly moved from one parish to another within a Union. Also by this Act you could not be removed after living one year in a parish.

Eventually these changes did allow labourers to move more freely about the country. But at first the New Poor Law had a surprising and unfortunate effect. Because it put more people onto the free labour market (those who had survived on allowances before) wages, far from rising as the commission had expected, actually fell in some parts. The poor suffered severely, and women and children were forced out into the fields to work, in order to raise enough money to live on.

The Act did achieve certain things. It cut the cost of poor relief; it slowly ended the allowance system and its bad effect on labourers' morale; and it laid the foundations for our modern local government system. But it had little to offer the unemployed industrial worker and it did nothing to make labour move freely, and so help Britain in the painful change from an agricultural to an industrial nation. To the other major problem of industrialisation, the foul living conditions in towns, Chadwick was to devote the rest of his life.

5 The Health of the People

Chadwick's interest in people's health grew while he was Secretary to the Poor Law Commissioners. So when the Commissioners allowed him to do less and less work in administering the Poor Law, he became more and more interested in public health. He noticed that sickness was one of the most common causes of poverty. If a man was off work because of sickness he earned no money. So he and his family had to apply to the parish for poor relief or starve.

Chadwick realised that the cost of the poor rates could be reduced if only sickness could be avoided—or prevented. And he believed the way to prevent sickness was to clear away the dirt and filth in the towns.

Unfortunately, the law stated that the poor rates could only be spent on relieving poverty. They could not be spent on preventing sickness, even though this might mean that the amount which had to be spent on poor relief was lower. Chadwick thought this was silly. He thought that if he could show that filth caused disease he could make the government see that it was actually cheaper to spend money on preventing people from becoming sick than on giving them poor relief after they became sick and unable to work.

The First Survey
In 1838 he got permission for a special survey. He arranged for three doctors, Kay, Arnott and Southwood Smith to investigate how the labouring classes lived in east London. When their reports were published they showed clearly that many of the diseases from which the working people suffered were caused by the filthy conditions in which they lived and the lack of

ventilation in their houses. The reports also showed that these diseases could be prevented by clearing away the rubbish, providing decent water supplies and better ventilation.

The report came as a great shock to many middle class people who had not known how terrible living conditions were for working people in big towns, because they never went near where the poor lived. Chadwick also realised from this report that the problem of public health was much bigger than even he had thought and much more important. He decided that there was a need for a large-scale investigation into the rest of the country to find out how poor people lived and what could be done to improve their way of life.

By this time many people were beginning to realise that the towns were a major problem. Because the population was growing rapidly, because many immigrants were coming into the country, particularly from Ireland, and because people were leaving the land to find work in the towns, the towns in the early nineteenth century were growing at a fantastic rate. Between 1801 and 1841 London doubled in size; from nearly one million inhabitants to nearly two million. In only ten years, between 1821 and 1831, Manchester and Salford increased by 47 per cent and in the same period Bradford grew by 78 per cent.

Back-to-back houses in Burnley

As a result, more and more people were crammed into the towns in increasingly insanitary conditions. At this time there were few building regulations. So builders were often free to get as many houses as they could on a site and to build them as cheaply as possible. They built houses in long rows, back to back, with no lavatories, drains or running water. Often there was an outside *privy* for every ten or twenty houses and water had to be fetched from a tap in the street. Usually there were no sewers under the streets in the poor parts of town and nobody to clean the streets either. As you can imagine, towns like this were very filthy indeed. The houses were also very crowded. Often a family of six or more had only one room and the cellars were let as separate dwellings. In 1847 Church Lane, in one of the worst areas in London, had 1,095 people living in 27 houses, an average of 40 people per house or 8 per room.

Chadwick's Survey and Report
At the time nobody really knew whether these conditions were widespread throughout Britain. It was to find out that Chadwick wanted an investigation. So in August 1839 Chadwick's friend, the Bishop of London, proposed a motion in the House of Lords that there should be an inquiry to see if the filthy living conditions which Kay, Arnott and Southwood Smith had found in London existed in other parts of the country. The motion was passed, and Chadwick was put in charge of the inquiry.

For the investigation Chadwick mainly used the Medical Officers of the Poor Law Unions and the Assistant Commissioners. He sent off long questionaires to these officials asking for detailed information about their areas. Chadwick followed this up by personally inspecting the worst areas and talking to the key witnesses. These inquiries covered the whole country, both towns and rural areas, including Scotland, and took two years.

When the 'Report on the Sanitary Condition of the Labouring Population' was completed in 1842 a crisis developed. The Poor Law Commissioners, who were officially responsible for the inquiry, refused to let the Report be published because they 47 thought it would cause too much trouble with bodies like the Metropolitan Commissions of Sewers, who were severely criticised in it. Eventually they compromised and the Report was issued under Chadwick's own name, so throwing the whole responsibility for it onto him. As it happened, this did Chadwick a lot of good because the Report was an enormous success and the credit went to him alone. Over 10,000 copies were distributed free to politicians, journalists and officials who might influence public opinion. Another 20,000 copies of the popular edition were sold. This made the Report a best seller. It was widely reviewed and praised in the Press, and quickly recognised as a great social document.

Chadwick begins the Report by stressing the enormous size of the problem. So many people died each year from epidemic and *contagious* diseases that, Chadwick said, 'the effect is as if the whole county of Westmorland now containing 56,469 souls, were entirely depopulated annually, and were occupied again by the growth of a new and feeble population living under the fears of a similar visitation.'

The major part of the Report is devoted to proving that where there is no drainage, poor water supply and overcrowding, there will also be disease, a high death rate and a short life. The fact that this seems so obvious now is a direct result of the public health movement which this Report

A filthy spot in South London—notice the rubbish tip and the pool of stagnant water

A family living in a cellar. They are about to be thrown out for not paying the rent

helped to establish. In the Report, Chadwick devotes page after page to printing reports from the Poor Law Medical Officers which hammer home this point. Here is how William Rayner, Medical Officer of the Heaton Norris district of Stockport describes his area:

'The localities in which fever mostly resides in my district, are Shepherd's Buildings and Back Water Street, both in the township of Heaton Norris. Shepherd's Buildings consist of two rows of houses with a street seven yards wide between them; each row consists of what are styled back and front houses—that is, the houses placed back to back. There are no yards or out conveniences; the privvies are in the centre of each row, about a yard wide; over them there is part of a sleeping room; there is no ventilation in the bedrooms; each house contains two rooms, viz, a house place and sleeping room above; each room is about three yards wide and four yards long. In one of these houses there are nine persons belonging to one family, and the mother on the eve of her confinement. There are 44 houses in the two rows, and 22 cellars, all of the same size. The cellars are let off as separate dwellings; these are dark, damp, and very low, not more than six feet between the ceiling and floor. The street between the two rows is seven yards wide, in the centre of which is the common gutter, into which all sorts of refuse is thrown; it is a foot in depth. Thus there is always a quantity of *putrefying* matter *contaminating* the air. At the end of the rows is a pool of water very shallow and stagnant, and a few yards further, a part of the town's gasworks. In many of these dwellings there are four persons in each bed.'

Living in a area like this was, of course, very unhealthy. Just how unhealthy few people had realised until Chadwick's Report. This table, from the Report, shows the average age at death of three classes of people in a rural area, Rutlandshire, and in one of the worst of the big towns, Manchester.

	Average age of death	
	In Manchester	*In Rutlandshire*
Professional persons and gentry and their families	38	52
Tradesmen and their families (In R. farmers and graziers are included with shopkeepers)	20	41
Mechanics, labourers and their families	17	38

Notice that you stood a very much better chance of living a long life in the country than in the town and that if you were a labourer in the town you were very much more likely to die early than if you were a lawyer. Of course these figures do not mean that no labourers in Manchester lived beyond the age of seventeen. They are average figures, and in fact show that a great many people died while they were very young. At this time in Manchester every other working class child died before the age of five.

The Problem of Refuse

One of the main reasons for this unhealthy state of affairs was that there were no means of getting rid of the rubbish and filth that are bound to exist in towns. There were no drains from the

Edward Edwards' trade card—the nightman cleaned out the cesspools, usually at night

houses to the sewers, except in some wealthy areas. People had to use *cesspools*. Very often there were no sewers anyway, except under the main streets, and those which existed were very inefficient. Finally, the rubbish in the streets was swept up by hand and carried away in carts, but again this only happened in the main streets. The results of this can easily be imagined, but this is how Dr. Duncan described one of the unhealthy courts in Liverpool.

'. . . finding that not less than 63 cases of fever had occurred in one year in Union-court, Banastre-Street, (containing twelve houses) I visited the court in order to ascertain, if possible, their origin, and I found the whole court *inundated* with fluid filth which had oozed through the walls from two adjoining ash-pits or cess-pools, and which

Houses in Preston with an open cesspool running between them

had no means of escape in consequence of the court being below the level of the street, and having no drain. The court was owned by two different landlords, one of whom had offered to construct a drain provided the other would join him in the expense; but this offer having been refused, the court had remained for two or three years in the state in which I saw it.'

Chadwick was able to show that the system of retaining refuse in cesspools was very dangerous to people's health. It was also expensive, since the cesspools had to be emptied by hand and the contents taken away in carts. In its place, Chadwick suggested that all houses should be fitted with drains so that the refuse could be flushed directly into the sewers. This would be both healthier and cheaper.

Lack of Sewers

Chadwick then pointed out that the sewers which existed were built on the wrong principles. At this time sewers were big enough for a man to work in; they had flat sides which tended to cave in; they were built of brick and had flat bottoms. So even when they were built with the right slope, the water flowing over the wide flat bottoms of *porous* brick could not sweep away the rubbish. As a result a thick deposit formed on the bottom and every five or ten years the street was ripped up and men had to climb in and shovel the muck into carts. These sewers were expensive to build and inefficient.

In their place Chadwick, with the help of some sanitary engineers, suggested a new system using narrow egg-shaped pipes of glazed pottery. In these, the water would be forced through the narrow smooth pipes and carry away all the refuse. They would never need cleaning by hand and Chadwick even suggested that the liquid manure which resulted could be piped out of town and used by farmers on the land. In fact nothing came of this last idea because while Chadwick was experimenting with methods of distribution, others discovered that artificial fertilisers were much more effective than sewage. This suggestion of 'pipe-drains' was a different matter. They were a third cheaper to build and lay than the old kind of drain and are in fact the models for those we use today. In spite of opposition from engineers who thought they were too fragile and would become easily blocked, 2,600 miles of 'pipe-drains' were laid by 1853.

Chadwick was really suggesting a complete new system of town drainage. He called it an 'arterial' system because it worked in a circle like the blood stream. Everything depended on water. Water would be pumped into the houses and after use leave the houses by drains flushing with it the household refuse. The drains would be connected to the main sewers and here again water was needed to break down the solid matter and carry it all away suspended in liquid. The streets too could be kept clean by sweeping the rubbish into the sewers and carrying it away with water.

Lack of Water
An adequate supply of water was, however, the second major problem. Chadwick found that the supply of water was quite inadequate. Only a few houses in wealthy districts had water piped in to the house. Most people had to collect their water

Queuing for water at a standpipe in the street. What are they using to collect water in?

from taps or pumps in the street, and store it in whatever pans or buckets they had in the house. Also at this time water was not constantly 'on tap.' It was only supplied by the Water Companies for two or three hours each day. As a result water was very precious, and only used for making tea, sometimes for cooking, and very seldom for washing. This is how the Rev. Whitworth Elwin described the situation in the poorer parts of Bath, a city which was better supplied with water than most:

'A man had to fetch water from one of the public pumps in Bath, the distance from his house being about a quarter of a mile,—"it is as valuable" he said "as strong beer. We can't use it for cooking or anything of that sort, but only for drinking and tea." "Then where do you get water for cooking and washing?" "Why from the river. But it is muddy, and often stinks bad, because all the filth is carried there." '

Water was usually supplied to towns by Water Companies, which were public companies with shareholders and Boards, who aimed to make a profit. These Water Companies either competed with each other, which was very wasteful since a particular street might have the pipes of two or three water companies running down it, or else they divided up a town, as they did in London, and so had a monopoly. Either way water was expensive. For this reason Chadwick was very interested in Bath where water was mainly supplied by the Corporation, very cheaply and efficiently.

Another problem was that houses were not built with piped water ready installed. It was left to individual owners or tenants to have water brought in if they wanted it. Of course this meant that the poor people could never afford it, particularly as they moved lodgings frequently, and landlords saw no reason to spend extra money on putting in water. Chadwick realised that the only solution was to make the local government authority responsible for the water system. The local authority could then install water in every house and charge tenants a small water rate. Naturally the Water Companies opposed this suggestion violently and it was many years before something like it was introduced.

Lack of Ventilation

The third main cause of disease, particularly diseases of the lung, was bad ventilation. At this time consumption, or tuberculosis as it is now usually called, was the most important single killer. It may have accounted for as many as a third of all deaths. Yet it was not generally realised that a constant supply of clean fresh air is as necessary to health as clean water and food. Air in the big towns was neither clean nor fresh. It was polluted by the stench from cesspools, sewers and rotting rubbish, as well as by the smoke from factories and houses. Fresh   55

A court in London—a woman is tipping her rubbish into the open drain in the middle of the court

A shoemaker's workshop

air could not circulate properly because the houses were built so close together in courts and narrow streets. In the houses it was even worse. Often a room would have only one small window which was kept tightly closed all winter to keep out the cold. The back-to-back houses were particularly bad because the solid wall which divided the front house from the back prevented any through ventilation. You can imagine what the air was like in a room where a family of six cooked, ate, slept and lived. The smell was unbelievable and germs thrived.

In the factories and places of work, ventilation was often just as bad. Some of the worst cases existed in the small shops of tailors and seamstresses. This is how Mr. Thomas Brownlow, a tailor, described his place of work in the Report.

'The place at which we used to work at Mr. Allen's was a room where 80 men worked together. It was a room 16 or 18 yards long and 7 or 8 yards wide, lighted with skylights: the men were close together, nearly knee to knee. In summer time the heat of the men and the heat of the irons made the room twenty or thirty degrees higher than the heat outside: The heat was then most suffocating, especially after the candles were lighted . . . the men sat as loosely as they could, and the perspiration ran from them from the heat and the closeness.'

Working under these conditions was terribly tiring and unhealthy. In order to keep going during the day the tailors at Mr. Allen's shop drank gin or beer for breakfast at seven and again at eleven, three, and five p.m. The long-term effects on their health were disastrous. It was very rare to find a man of fifty still able to work, and many died of consumption long before then. Chadwick looked into the cause of death of 233 tailors in the Eastern and Western Unions of London in 1839. He found that 123 had died from diseases of the *respiratory* system (92 of those from consumption), 16 from diseases of the nervous system, 16 from epidemic or contagious diseases, 8 from diseases of the digestive system, 23 were uncertain, and only 29 had died of 'old age'.

Lack of ventilation, lack of water and lack of proper drainage were the main reasons for the appalling condition in which the labouring classes lived. There were, of course, others. Wages were generally low, so that it was difficult to get enough to eat. Food was often terrible. Meat—when you could afford it—might be bad, and cheating shopkeepers mixed fine brown earth with the cocoa and chalk with the flour. Bad houses undoubtedly drove both men and women to drink far too much. In Glasgow in 1840 there was said to be one public house for every ten dwelling houses. Because women were employed so much in factories, children were often grossly neglected. The women themselves knew little about cooking and keeping house, because they had been at work since the age of ten, so they probably spent the little money they had very badly.

Of course it would be a mistake to think that all the working

A cartoon called "The Bottle"

people lived like this. Many undoubtedly managed to keep themselves clean, healthy and reasonably well fed. But Chadwick's Report did show that for the labouring population as a whole life was very unhealthy, much more unhealthy than people had realised. 'The annual loss of life,' wrote Chadwick, 'from filth and bad ventilation are greater than the loss from death or wounds in any wars in which this country has been engaged in modern times.'

Should the Government Interfere?
The Report is also important because it showed that middle class people were quite wrong in thinking that the miserable circumstances of the poor were their own fault, the result of bad character. There was in fact very little that the poor could do to help themselves. This is very important because it helped to get across the idea that the State would have to intervene in order to improve the public's health. Today, we are quite used to the State telling us what is good for our health, but in 1842 people were not. Most people then believed that the government should interfere as little as possible. But ideas were changing. People were beginning to realise that, in a crowded little island, it was no longer possible to leave everyone free to do what he liked.

The whole effect of Chadwick's Report is to make it seem right that the government should interfere in order to protect the lives of the people. This message is summed up by Dr. William Davidson, senior physician at Glasgow Royal Infirmary, whose passionate plea for intervention Chadwick printed in the Report. 'The evil will continue to *assail* us so long as our cities contain so many narrow and filthy lanes, so long as the houses situated there are little better than dens or hovels, so long as dunghills and other nuisances are allowed to accumulate in their *vicinity*, so long as these hovels are crowded with inmates, and so long as there is so much poverty and destitution.

'Why, then, should we not have a law that would level these hovels to the ground—that would regulate the width of every street—that would regulate the ventilation of every dwelling house—that would prevent the lodging houses of the poor from being crowded with human beings, and that would provide for destitution? It may be said that this would interfere too much with the liberty of the subject, and no doubt it would be vehemently opposed by many interested persons. In place, however, of being an *infringement* on the liberty of the subject, it might rather be *designated* an attempt to prevent the improper liberties of the subject: for what right, moral or constitutional, has any man to form streets, construct houses, and crowd them with human beings so as to deteriorate health and shorten life, because he finds it profitable to do so?'

6   Burying the Dead

As soon as Chadwick's 'Sanitary Report' was published the Home Secretary asked him to investigate another urgent health problem—that of burial in towns. Chadwick threw himself into this with his usual energy and published the results of his inquiries in 1843 as a supplement to his 'Sanitary Report.'

Burial in Towns

Today, most people are either buried in large cemeteries or cremated. In 1842 most people were buried in churchyards, just as they still are in country villages. You can imagine that, as the towns grew rapidly in size, there simply was not room in the small churchyards for all the people who had to be buried. In London the problem was particularly bad. Here is how Chadwick described the situation in his Report:

'In the metropolis, on spaces of ground which do not exceed 203 acres, closely surrounded by the abodes of the living, layer upon layer, each consisting of a population numerically equivalent to a large army of 20,000 adults and nearly 30,000 youths and children is every year imperfectly interred [buried].'

These small overcrowded cemeteries surrounded by houses were desperately unhealthy. Chadwick believed that the gas from decaying bodies caused disease. In fact this is not so, however unpleasant it may be. But these graveyards did contaminate the water supply and spread disease that way. The overcrowding was also very offensive to people's sense of respect for the dead. Again Chadwick describes the effect.

'In the common graveyards in the metropolis the bones are scattered about, or wheeled away to a bone-house, where

A burial in progress at a churchyard in the Strand, London

they are thrown into a heap. The feeling of the labouring classes at the sight of the removal of the bones from an overcrowded churchyard was expressed in a recent complaint, that those in charge of the place 'would not give the poor bones time to decay'.'

The graveyards were unhealthy enough. An even worse cause of disease was the habit of keeping the body in the house for several days before burying it. John Liddle, Medical Officer for Whitechapel in London, was asked to describe the practice. 'On the occurrence of death amongst most labourers, how is the corpse dealt with?'

'Nearly the whole of the labouring population have only one room. The corpse is therefore kept in that room where the inmates sleep and have their meals. Sometimes the corpse is stretched on the bed, and the bedclothes are taken off, and the wife and family lie on the floor. Sometimes it is stretched out on chairs.'

'What is the usual length of time that the corpse is so left?'

A dead body kept in a family's only room – it is under a sheet on a mattress on the floor

'The time varies according to the day of the death. Sunday is the day usually chosen for the day of burial. But if a man dies on a Wednesday, the burial will not take place till the Sunday week following. Bodies are almost always kept for a full week, frequently longer.'

Where death had occurred from contagious diseases such as cholera, the result of keeping the body in such a room for a week or more can be easily imagined. The Report has many accounts of people who died from this practice.

There were several reasons for this delay. People were terrified of burying their relatives before they were really dead, and so waited several days to make sure. This is more understandable when you remember that usually no medical officer was called to check on the cause of death. Sunday was chosen for burials so that the family would not lose money by missing a working day. But much the commonest reason given for this delay was that families needed time to raise enough money for a proper funeral. Funeral expenses were a great burden even on the well-to-do 63 classes at this time, but they were even more so on the labouring classes. The average minimum charge for a funeral was about £5, and this provided a stout elm coffin, bearers to carry the corpse to the grave, and some fittings (gloves, crepe bands) for the mourners. Imagine how difficult it must have been to raise such a sum at a time when 10 shillings a week was thought to be a decent wage for an unskilled labourer.

The Cost of Burials
Chadwick believed that these costs were much higher than they need be. In fact, he reckoned that they could be reduced by half. He noticed that when someone has died the family is not in a position to argue about the funeral. No one wants to seem mean at such a time, and often an undertaker would simply be told to lay on 'what is usual.' Also, there were far too many people trying to make a living out of undertaking. Here is how Chadwick described the situation in London.

> 'The number of deaths per day in the metropolis is, on an average of three years, 114. The number of people whose sole business is that of undertaker, whose names are *enumerated* in the Post Office Directory for the year 1843 is 265. Besides these there are 258 'undertakers and carpenters' 34 'undertakers and upholsterers,' 56 'undertakers and appraisers,' 19 'undertakers and auctioneers,' 7 'undertakers and house agents,' 3 'undertakers and fancy cabinet makers,' 2 'undertakers and and packing-case makers,' making in all no less than 730 persons for 114 deaths.'

Obviously with this number of people trying to make a living out of undertaking many firms were doing less than one funeral a week. So their charges would have to be high if they were to make enough money.

Finding the Money
Those who were better paid tried to cover the funeral expenses by some form of insurance, or out of the savings which they deposited in the savings banks. The lowest paid workers usually belonged to a burial club. Members of these burial clubs paid in a penny or twopence a week and on death the burial club paid out between £5 and £10 (£3 for a child). In all the big towns

there were many of these clubs, often quite small. Because they were small they sometimes failed. Fearing that their club might fail led people to subscribe to more than one club. Inevitably this was too much of a temptation for some people. A number, particularly children, were killed for the burial money, which, because it came from several clubs, would be much more than was needed for the funeral. This was all the easier to do since no medical officer had to verify the cause of death. Here is the description in Chadwick's Report of a case in Manchester which came to light because Mr. Gardiner, the clerk to the Union, became suspicious about the cause of death.

'The child had been entered in at least ten burial clubs; and its parents had six other children, who only lived from nine to eighteen months respectively. They had received £20 from several burial clubs for one of these children, and they expected to receive at least as much on account of this child. An inquest was held at Mr. Gardiner's insistence, when several persons who had known the deceased stated that she was a fine fat child shortly after her birth, but that she soon became quite thin, was badly clothed, and seemed as if she did not get a sufficiency of food.'

Bunhill Fields, London,—this drawing was made several years after burials had been stopped in it but you can see how overcrowded it was.

Chadwick's Recommendations

At the end of his 200-page report Chadwick listed the remedies which he wanted to see introduced. At the time they must have seemed very revolutionary, yet many of them have since been accepted. First, he suggested that burial in churches and churchyards within towns should be stopped. In their place Chadwick wanted a system of national public cemeteries built outside the town limits where everyone could be buried 'at reduced and moderate prices, suitable to the station of the deceased.' Secondly, he suggested that medical officers of health should be appointed who would have to verify the fact and cause of all deaths. They would also have the power to take action when death was caused by a disease which might harm the survivors. This was to guard against the fear of premature burial, murders and starving of children, and the dangers of keeping an infectious body in the house.

7 The Board of Health

The Health of Town's Commission

Chadwick's two reports had created so much interest and discussion that the Government clearly had to do something. But this was a quite new field for Government action and they were naturally cautious. They announced a Royal Commission. It was to examine the state of 50 of the largest towns and test Chadwick's recommendations. When it reported in July 1844 and February 1845 it confirmed Chadwick's findings. This is hardly surprising when we learn from Chadwick that 'though not named in the Commission, the Commissioners having their own occupation to pursue, I was compelled to attend to it, write their questions, take the examinations, and prepare their Report'. He also persuaded the Commissioners to follow his own practice of going to see for themselves. Those who were not as

Lord Shaftesbury visiting a London slum

tough as Chadwick had a rough time. 'My vacation has been absorbed' he wrote, 'in visiting, with Mr. Smith and Dr. Playfair the worst parts of some of the worst towns. Dr. Playfair has been knocked up by it and has been seriously ill. Mr. Smith has had a little dysentry. Sir Henry de la Beche was obliged at Bristol to stand up at the end of alleys and vomit while Dr. Playfair was investigating overflowing privies. Sir Henry was obliged to give it up.'

The Health of Towns Act 1848

Once the Royal Commission had reported, no Government could avoid the need to act. At the same time public opinion was roused by the Health of Towns Association which was formed in December 1844 with a powerful committee, including the Bishop of London, Disraeli, and Lord Shaftesbury. In spite of this, attempts to introduce a Public Health Bill were pushed aside in the crisis over the repeal of the Corn Laws, and it was nearly four years later, that in 1848 the first Public Health Act was passed by Parliament. The Bill, which was introduced by Lord Morpeth had met a good deal of opposition in parliament, and when passed it was not nearly so strong a law as Chadwick had wanted. It set up for five years only a Board of Health of three people—a member of the Government, Lord Morpeth, as Chairman, one full-time paid Commissioner, Chadwick, and one unpaid Commissioner, Lord Shaftesbury. Later, a fourth medical commissioner, Dr. Southwood Smith, was added. The Board could only intervene to set up a local board of health in places where the death rate exceeded 23 per 1,000. Otherwise, it could only set up local boards where 10 per cent of the ratepayers signed a petition to have the Act applied. Where a local board of health was set up, it had power to impose a special rate to pay for improvement schemes. But the schemes had first to be approved by the general Board of Health. This gave the Board considerable power to prevent local boards from doing anything which it did not approve of, but the Board of Health could not compel the local boards to introduce improvement schemes.

Along with the Public Health Act, Parliament passed a Nuisances Removal Act, which could be brought into effect in times of national epidemics, and was intended to give the Board of Health special powers to deal with such emergencies. This Act was rushed through Parliament to meet the threat of the most feared epidemic of all—cholera. Almost as soon as the Board of Health was set up, it was having to grapple with the second major assault of this fearful disease. Cholera had first swept across Europe from India in 1831 reaching Great Britain in 1832, where it killed 21,000 people in England and Wales, 9,000 in Scotland, and a further 20,000 in Ireland. No cure was found for it, and it struck particularly hard in the filthy homes of the poor. As the second wave moved across Europe all the old terrors revived. People feared particularly the speed with which cholera struck, sometimes killing within a few hours, and the frightening symptoms. This is how these symptoms were described by the temporary Board of Health in 1832.

'Vomiting or purging come on; the features become sharp and contracted, the eye sinks; the lips, face, neck, hands and feet and soon after the thighs, arms, and whole surface assume a leaden, blue, purple, black or deep brown tint; the pulse becomes small as a thread or else totally extinct. The skin is deadly cold, the tongue flabby and chilled like a piece of dead flesh. The patient speaks in a whisper. He struggles for breath. Sometimes there are rigid spasms of the legs, thighs and loins.'

The illustration on page 70 shows one of the earliest cholera victims in England.

As soon as the Board had been formed in September 1848 there was a rush of work to issue regulations to the Boards of Guardians about the approaching cholera. They were to take immediate steps to prevent the cholera getting a grip by removing all unhealthy 'nuisances' in their areas. If cholera did strike, they were to appoint medical inspectors to organise house-to-house inspection of the likely fever spots. Where they found cases they were to remove the healthy to Houses of Refuge which were also to be set up.

Immediately, the weakness of the Board's powers became obvious. It could not make the Guardians do what it wanted. Very few Boards of Guardians took any measures of prevention and even when cholera had struck their areas many Boards, particularly in London, still refused to act. Not a single Union in London tried to search out cholera victims in their homes, and only three Unions set up Houses of Refuge. As the attack got sharply worse in August 1849, the Board decided to organise the house-to-house visiting itself, and got leave to appoint a medical inspector and four assistants. These started on the worst districts and the Board ordered the Guardians to appoint medical visitors and put the Union medical staff at its disposal. Reluctantly, most of them complied. By now, deaths in London had reached a peak of 2,000 in a week and the graveyards were overflowing. Again the Board took the law into its own hands and ordered the worst graveyards to be closed. Again some of the parishes refused to obey, and when the cases went before the judges the Board lost. By then, however, the worst was over, and within a month the cholera had subsided. But, when the

A Court for King Cholera – a famous cartoon from Punch

deaths were counted, it was found that 53,000 had died in England and Wales, 7,000 in Scotland, and 30,000 in Ireland.

The Board could not have started at a more difficult time, but it had tackled the problem vigorously. Public opinion was very much on its side. Chadwick, Southwood Smith, and a number of the officials had been struck down with fevers but had hurried back to their work while most other people who could fled London. The Board had been able to do most good where its inspectors arrived in time and were able to persuade local authorities to act. Even so, most of the good was done by accident, since the Board had really no idea how cholera worked. They believed, quite wrongly, that cholera was not a contagious disease, passed on by contact between people, but something in the atmosphere caused by dirt and filth. Chadwick put this idea most forcefully when he said 'All smell is disease.' This ignorance may seem surprising but we should remember that no one else understood cholera and it was to be another 35 years before the German scientist Robert Koch discovered in the cholera bacillus (a tiny germ), the true cause of the disease.   71

The appalling conduct of the London Guardians and church vestries made Chadwick more than ever determined to tackle the problem of London's health. The Public Health Act deliberately did not cover London, although it was much the largest city and one of the filthiest. This was mainly because there was no single authority which could administer the Act. London was simply a geographical expression. It was not one town, but literally hundreds of different parishes, Unions, improvement commissions, all with different boundaries and all working under local Acts. When the vicar of Christ Church, Regents Park, enquired about the procedure for cleansing his parish, he was told 'In the parish of St. Pancras, where you reside, there are no less than sixteen separate paving boards, acting under twenty-nine Acts of Parliament, all of which would have to be consulted.' Sewerage for the Metropolitan area was looked after by no less than eight Commissions, with a total of 1,065 Commissioners. Water was supplied by eight private companies. Chadwick was appalled by this muddle, and hated the vestries, water companies and Commissions of Sewers. '*Sinister* interests' he called them, and was determined not to leave London's health in their hands. In their place, Chadwick wanted a single Crown-appointed Commission which would be responsible for the whole Metropolis, as London was then called. This body would be responsible for all paving, lighting and cleaning. It would take over sewerage from the Commissions of Sewers, and water supply from the private companies, and of course, it would need to be able to impose rates on all householders. Here lay the root of the problem— under no circumstances would the vestries agree to be taxed by a Commission on which they were not represented. It is important to understand this problem, because the opposition of the Metropolitan vestries and members of Parliament was later a key reason for the failure of the Board of Health.

Chadwick's scheme for the Metropolis is typical of his whole way of dealing with these problems. As with the Poor Law, so with London's health, he studied the jumble of existing practices and then came up with a solution which did away with all of them and imposed a new system, simple, logical and complete. But it paid no attention to how people were then prepared to be governed, and immediately provoked bitter hostility. Over the next five years all Chadwick's plans for London were defeated.

London's Drainage

As a start, the Government agreed to abolish the eight Commissions of Sewers, and appoint a single Metropolitan Commission of Sewers. Chadwick and the other members of the Board of Health were appointed to this together with some representatives of the vestries. In a short time the Commission was so bitterly divided over Chadwick's plans for the main drainage that eventually the Government had to intervene, dismiss all the Commissioners, and start again with a fresh lot. After this, Chadwick could only agitate from the sidelines. The discussions about London's main drainage dragged on and on, and it was 1865 before London finally got a main drainage system.

The Prince of Wales starting the engines at the opening of London's main drainage works in 1865

London's Cemeteries

While people could still remember the state of the burial grounds during the cholera epidemic, Chadwick produced an equally ambitious scheme for reforming burial practice in London. Under this plan, the General Board of Health was to take over all the burials in the Metropolis, close the churchyards, buy up the new commercial burial grounds, and open new ones outside the town's limits. In spite of opposition from the vestries, this plan passed the Commons easily and became law in 1850. It is doubtful whether the Government had really understood what was involved. Only gradually did they realise that because the Board would have to pay a vast sum to buy up the cemeteries and compensate the clergy for taking away burial fees, it could only afford to do this if it had a complete monopoly of all burials. This was too much for the Government, and in 1852 a new Act was passed which took away the overall responsibility from the Board of Health and gave the Home Secretary power to close offensive burial grounds. It also gave individual parishes the power to acquire new grounds outside the built-up areas. In the next year, the Act was extended to the rest of the country and at last the worst burial grounds started to be closed.

London's Water

By 1850 the Board had completed its investigations into the water supply of London. The situation was certainly dreadful. Water supply was in the hands of eight profit-making companies. At first, there had been intense and very wasteful competition. 'There were in some streets three distinct sets of pipes. *Capricious* customers were constantly changing from one set to the other, and the pavement was torn up daily. The plumbers' bills were of course enormous. So sharp was the practice that sometimes the pipes were put to the wrong main, and one company sent in the bill for water which its opponent had unconsciously supplied.' After this the companies agreed to combine together and put up their prices. Even so, the service was very bad. Houses in the rich areas were well served, but 70,000 houses were supplied in groups of 20 or 30 by stand-pipes in the street, which were only on for an hour a day, three days a week. Houses south of the Thames were supplied by companies who drew their water from the Thames, into which 237 public sewers were emptied. Only three companies filtered their water and their reservoirs were uncovered. This Punch cartoon shows what Londoners thought of this situation.

DIPHTHERIA.   SCROFULA.   CHOLERA.

ATHER THAMES INTRODUCING HIS OFFSPRING TO THE FAIR CITY OF LONDON.

Under the Board's plan no more water would be drawn from the Thames. They had found a new source in Surrey. The existing water companies were to be joined together into one, and water supply along with main drainage put in the hands of a Government-appointed Board. But this plan was much too far-reaching for the Government, and even the Bill which they

75

The filtering basins of the Lambeth Water Company's new works at Ditton–opened after the Act of 1852

did introduce to consolidate the water companies met such fierce opposition that it had to be withdrawn. Eventually, in 1852 a new Act was passed which allowed the separate companies to continue, but insisted that they should not draw water from the Thames below Teddington Lock, and should cover their reservoirs and filter their water. The water companies kept going until 1901, when they were bought out for the enormous sum of £43 million.

In the Rest of the Country

While Chadwick was fighting and losing this long battle for London's health, he and the rest of the Board were also busy at work at their main responsibility—applying the Public Health Act to the rest of England. This was the procedure. As soon as the Board received a petition from one tenth of the ratepayers it gave the town 14 days warning that one of its inspectors was coming to make an enquiry. The enquiry was held in public, and the Inspector's report and recommendations were published. There was then one month for people to object to the Report, and if any serious objections were made there was a further enquiry. After these enquiries the Board could decide to enforce the Act, which was then operated either by the local corporation, or by a specially elected Board. The local authority could impose rates and borrow money for major schemes, such as drainage, but these had to be approved by the Board of Health.

This way of working was a great improvement on the earlier system whereby each town had to get its own Private Bill passed through Parliament. The new system was much cheaper. It cost, on average, £112 to apply the Act, when Private Bills cost between £1,600 and £2,000. It was also quick, and provided a reasonable chance for public discussion. The Board kept in reserve its powers to enforce the Act when the death rate was over 23 per 1,000. On the whole, the Act worked very well. By 1854 over 170 towns had set up local Boards, and these included some major towns such as Bristol, Bradford, Wolverhampton, Wakefield and Rotherham. The biggest towns of all, Liverpool, Manchester and Birmingham, however, all obtained Private Acts. Although there was not much organised opposition to the Act, it did create in each town in addition to a 'clean' party who supported the Act, a 'dirty' party who objected to the increased rates. Charles Dickens described their reactions like this: 'Ratepayers, Cess-cum-Poolton. Rally round your vested interests. Health is enormously expensive. Introduce the Public Health Act and be pauperised. Be filthy and be fat.'

Once a local Board had been set up, the success of the Public Health Act depended very much on their activity. In order to see what this meant in practice, we need to look in some detail at how the Act was applied in one town.

8 The Public Health Act in Practice – Darlington

Darlington was one of the first places to apply for the Act and is a good place to study for a number of reasons. In the 1850s it was a growing industrial town, with many of the problems of the big towns like Manchester and Birmingham. But it was still fairly compact. Its population in 1851 was 11,228. It had railways and woollen mills, and was a centre for the cattle trade with London. It was also one of the first places to appoint a Medical Officer of Health, and fortunately for us his first five annual reports have survived.

The Procedure

In February 1849 a group of local ratepayers sent a letter to the General Board of Health in London. They complained that 'the attempt which is now making to procure the signatures of one tenth of the inhabitants, so as to make application for the Health of Towns Act, is both *premature* and uncalled for, as the town was never in a more healthful state than it is at present.' They also said that they already had a Local Improvement Act and that the death rate was less than the required 23 per 1,000. They complained that it was 'oppressive' that one tenth could apply 'against the wish of the inhabitants at large', and that the Act would involve 'serious burthens' on the ratepayers and 'unnecessary expense.'

In spite of this, a petition was signed by one tenth of the ratepayers, and sent to the General Board of Health. The Board appointed Mr. William Ranger to carry out the investigation, and in October 1849 Mr. Ranger arrived in Darlington. He set up in the Central Hall and began to take evidence, particularly from the medical men in the town.

One of the most helpful was Stephen Edward Piper, Medical Officer to the Poor Law Union. William Ranger also went out to see what the town was like for himself.

Ranger's Report

By February 1850 Ranger's report was ready, and was presented to the Board of Health. As usual, the Board ordered it to be published and gave the people of Darlington until July to appeal against Ranger's findings. The report is a long one, over 70 pages, and gives us a very detailed picture of Darlington at that time.

The title page of Ranger's Report

PUBLIC HEALTH ACT,
(11 & 12 Vict., Cap. 63.)

REPORT

TO THE

GENERAL BOARD OF HEALTH,

ON A

PRELIMINARY INQUIRY

INTO THE SEWERAGE, DRAINAGE, AND SUPPLY OF
WATER, AND THE SANITARY CONDITION
OF THE INHABITANTS

OF THE TOWN OF

DARLINGTON,
IN THE COUNTY OF DURHAM.

BY WILLIAM RANGER, ESQ.,
SUPERINTENDING INSPECTOR.

LONDON:
PRINTED BY W. CLOWES & SONS, STAMFORD STREET,
FOR HER MAJESTY'S STATIONERY OFFICE.
1850.

First Ranger looked into the death rate. The average for the seven years to 1849 was 22.97 deaths per 1,000. But he found that this crude average figure hid the fact that in some parts of the town the death rate was much higher—in one street as high as 47 per 1,000. When he divided the town into its poorer and healthier halves, he found that the first had a death rate of 28 per 1,000 and the second only 17 per 1,000. 'Thus the inhabitants of some of the streets lose 17 years of their lives as compared with others,' he concluded, and also noted that in some streets two-thirds of the number of deaths were of children under five. Clearly, some parts of the town were very unhealthy.

This map is copied from the one in Ranger's report. It gives us a clue about the unhealthy parts of the town. Notice the wide main streets and the open space in the middle, which is the market. Then notice the groups of houses off the main streets, particularly the ones off Skinnergate. They do not follow any regular pattern, and often the houses are built on all four sides of narrow courts. These courts were the unhealthy parts of Darlington. Ranger found that the main streets were 'open and airy', 'macadamised and kept in tolerably good state of repair'. But these courts and side-streets were quite different. Very little air could get in because of the houses all round, and usually the courts were not paved so that there were pools of stagnant water. There were very few privvies—in some yards over 60 people had only one to use. Inside, the houses were even worse—no running water, no drains, no proper ventilation and dreadfully overcrowded. In one court Dr. Piper found '15 persons in two small rooms were ill at the same time of typhus fever, lying on the floor on straw, and I had to step over from one to another to attend them. There was no ventilation, and I broke three squares of glass to admit air.'

The town had scarcely any main drainage. Of the 56 streets and 106 courts, 13 streets were sewered, 18 streets were partly sewered, and 23 had none. 42 yards were drained, but 68 were not. Even the sewers which did exist were inefficient—some were square with stone sides and tops, but no bottoms; in some places brick drains 14 inches by 12 inches had been used where 3 inch pipe drains would have been enough, and none of the

Map of Darlington in 1850

sewers was deep enough to drain the cellars. This situation is not surprising when we learn that there was no single authority whose job it was to look after sewers. The sewers which existed had been put down by three separate sets of 'surveyors of the highway'—though legally they were not allowed to lay sewers and certainly not to use money from the highway rate as they had done.

The town's water supply was just about to change for the better. The Darlington Gas and Water Company was building a waterworks including two *filter beds* 80 feet by 50 feet and a service reservoir to hold 800,000 gallons of water. The water was being brought from the river Tees, and the company had offered to supply at 1d. per week to houses with yearly rents of less than £3. But until this started most people still got their water from wells— usually from public pumps in the streets or courts. The poor complained to Ranger that they had to go a long way to fetch water, and sometimes the wells were spoiled by soakage from the drains and cess-pits.

The streets were lighted by gas. There were 156 public lights at distances of 50 to 60 yards, which were kept burning from sunset to sunrise. The Darlington Gas and Water Company put up the lights and looked after them, including lighting them and putting them out. For this they were paid £387 19s. per year—quite a substantial item. By comparison, the town had spent a total of £35 on sewers in 1847.

The burial grounds were another major problem. There were three at this time. St. Cuthbert's, the parish church, was the main one, and was right in the centre of town (find it on the map). It was quite large, 2 acres and 38 perches, but was by now terribly overcrowded. 1,617 people had been buried in it in the last 7 years, and a churchwarden told Ranger 'the state of the old churchyard is disgraceful, immediate steps should be taken for closing it'. The other two burial grounds were no problem. Trinity was new (1843), and only 214 people had been buried there, while only 30 had been buried in the Friends' ground in the last 7 years. The estimated cost of burials in Darlington then was £40– £100 for the gentry and professional classes, £12 for the lower class of tradesman, and £4 for the labouring classes.

Finally, there were various sorts of nuisance. There was no system for collecting refuse from the streets and courts, except that once a fortnight 'one man and a horse, with a boy, are employed on the day following the holding of the cattle market.' There were no public conveniences, which must have been a problem on market days. There were about 30 butchers and 24 slaughterhouses in the town, usually in amongst the houses, and pigs were often kept in the courts.

Not surprisingly, in these poor social conditions, there was a lot of drunkenness. Ranger counted 50 public houses and 20 beer shops. He also discovered that in three months on the west

A view of Darlington in 1843, looking towards the Market Square with the Parish Church in the background

side of the town they brought in 933 gallons of brandy, 1,414 gallons of rum, 654 gallons of whiskey, and 2,048 gallons of gin. We don't know whether the same sort of amount came in on the east side, or whether it was all drunk in Darlington, but it seems an enormous quantity of liquor for a town of under 12,000 people.

Ranger ended his report by recommending that the Local Improvement Act should be *repealed,* since it was useless, and the Public Health Act applied. He suggested a local Board of Health of 18 people. He also suggested a number of ways in which the town could be made more healthy. First, a proper system of sewers should be laid down. Next, St. Cuthbert's burial ground should be closed and a new one opened outside the town in Staindrop Road. A public park was needed, so that labourers from the crowded courts could get some fresh air. Public baths and wash-houses should be built, so that labourers could clean more than their hands and faces occasionally, and do the family washing outside the one room they usually had to live in. The streets and courts should be paved and refuse cleared   83 away regularly. The houses of the poor should be drained, whitewashed and better ventilated; the cesspools should be closed and *water closets* provided. In all, it provided the Local Board of Health with a big programme of reform.

The Board Starts Work

The Local Board was duly elected in August 1850, and 15 of the 18 members attended the first meeting on 28 September. The election of members must have been quite lively, since the minute book has the names not only of the 18 elected members but of 56 other candidates as well. This first meeting was devoted to electing a Chairman, William Backhouse, and a Clerk, John Peacock, and the Board agreed to meet at least once a month at the Town Hall. Usually, they met more frequently. On 8 October, the Board agreed to advertise for a Collector of Rates, a Surveyor and an Inspector of Nuisances. By a lucky chance, a

A poster advertising the first appointments to be made by the Darlington Board of Health

DARLINGTON
LOCAL BOARD OF HEALTH.

The Board purpose at their next Meeting, to appoint the following Officers, viz:—

A COLLECTOR of Rates, a SURVEYOR, and an INSPECTOR of NUISANCES,

And will receive Written Proposals from Applicants.

The Collector will be required to find approved Security for £300.

The proposals for the Offices of Surveyor and Inspector of Nuisances, may be made to undertake them either together or separately.

Information as to the precise nature of the duties of each office may be obtained on *personal* application at my office, and sealed proposals stating the remuneration required, and indorsed " Application for the office of ———— to The Darlington Local Board of Health," (and in the case of the Collector with the names of the proposed Security) must be sent to me not later than Twelve o'clock at noon, on Thursday the 17th Instant.

The Board give no pledge to accept the lowest offers.

By order, JOHN S. PEACOCK,
CLERK TO THE BOARD.

Darlington, October 8th, 1850.

J. MANLEY, PRINTER, 41 HIGH ROW, DARLINGTON.

copy of this advertisement has survived and is printed here. Why do you think the Collector had to find 'approved security for £300'? On 18 October the Board considered the applications and appointed Hugh Dunn Collector of Rates at a salary of £25 per year. George Mason was appointed Surveyor at £40 a year, and also Inspector of Nuisances, at a further £10 a year. At this stage the jobs were not intended to occupy a man full time.

After this the Board quickly got down to business. It took over the accounts of the three separate Highway Surveyors and also the fire engine. The Surveyor reported on the state of the town, and the Board began to order things to be done—'that the Public Pumps be repaired and painted', 'that a drain in Boundsgate be made as suggested by the Surveyor'. The Board had considerable powers to approve plans for new houses, and to order improvements for existing streets and houses. For instance, on 8 December we find: 'Thos. Elvins House—Plans of this intended house are produced and leave is given to erect it as proposed—the ash pit to be covered.' On 23 January 1857, 'Bank Top Cut—Notice to the York, Newcastle and Berwick Railway Company to sewer, level, pave, *flag*, and channel this to the satisfaction of the Board is ordered to be prepared against the next meeting.' At the same meeting it was agreed 'that all existing privvies and ashpits be furnished with proper doors and coverings by 3rd March next and the Clerk do issue a Handbill accordingly.' Issuing orders was easy enough, but making sure these orders were obeyed was much more difficult, and in the end the Board depended on the Magistrates. For instance on 20 February the Board learnt that William Stobbart had failed to whitewash his houses in Palace Yard, and 'the Clerk is ordered to take proceedings on Saturday next for the recovery before the Magistrates of the Penalties incurred' (that is, Stobbart was to be fined).

As well as dealing with these smaller matters, the Board had also begun on some of the important recommendations in Ranger's report. On 5 December the Board agreed to draw up 'a complete plan of drainage and sewerage in accordance with the present most improved system'. On 16 October 1851 the

<u>Hackney carriages.</u>   The Subject of requiring the Proprietors of Hackney Carriages to be licensed and registered is again considered and the Board is of the opinion that the same is not necessary at present.

<u>Mr Furby's Houses.</u> }   The Surveyor produced a Plan of 2 Houses and outbuildings proposed to be erected by Mr Francis Furby in King Street Darlington and the same are approved subject to this condition viz That the Privies and Ashpits be covered in and that the grates in the footpath in front be constructed to the satisfaction of the Surveyor of this Board.

<u>Slaughter Houses</u>
and
<u>Lodging Houses.</u> }   The Officer of Health and the Inspector of Nuisances are requested to inspect and report upon the whole of the Slaughter Houses and Lodging Houses so soon as the Bye laws are received confirmed

Above: extract from the minute book of the Darlington Board of Health

Dr S. E. Piper

Board applied to the General Board of Health to begin legal proceedings to stop burials in St. Cuthbert's ground. On 30 October a committee was formed to look into the possibility of setting out a public park.

Dr Piper's Report

The Board's minute book gives us a sense of the vigour with which the Board tackled its job, but it is difficult to get a clear idea of what it was achieving. Fortunately, we can get this from another source. Dr. S. E. Piper was appointed Medical Officer of Health in December 1850 at a salary of £20 a year. He was already Medical Officer of the Poor Law Union, and a strong believer in sanitary reform. Each year until 1856, he presented a report to the Local Board on the town's health during that year. These reports have survived and through them we get a very clear picture of what was achieved at Darlington.

1851

Piper's first report, for the year 1851, backs up Ranger's comments on the town. He found the same contrast between the 'opulence, cleanliness, and comfort' of the best parts of town, and the poorer sections with their 'numerous dirty lanes, dark passages, narrow alleys and crowded courts and yards, undrained, badly paved, ill-supplied with air, light and water, where disgusting nuisances abound, which time after time have been reported as being ruinous to health, and prejudicial to the morals of the inhabitants'. The state of the river Skerne was particularly alarming: 'this sluggish and polluted stream ought not to be the open sewer for all the filth in Darlington.' So too was the state of the burial ground and Piper recommended that 'immediate steps should be taken to close this overcrowded graveyard'. He urged the need for a 'copious supply of water' which was now available from the Water Company, but the poor were still using the hard water from the wells or collecting their own in raintubs. He has a particularly nasty story about the raintubs. Apparently, a family in Boundsgate who had been using one of these found the water increasingly foul and opened up the rainbutt to discover 'the decomposing body of a child   87

which had been saturating there for a month'. But something
had been done. 'Excellent baths of various kinds have during the
past year been established and set up in the best possible
manner.' Unfortunately, the poor had not yet learned to use
these. Even so, he urged the need to provide wash-houses as
well, so that the poor would not have to sit 'amidst the *nauseous*
smells of half-washed linen and steaming soap-suds'.

1852

In 1852 conditions were still bad. The population had now
risen to 11,600 and 288 people died that year, an average of 25
per 1,000. More than a third of the deaths (109) were from
diseases like typhus and dysentery, which thrive on dirty
conditions. In one particularly bad part of town, in the group
of houses east of the river Skerne between Park Street and
Skerne Row, the death rate was a fantastic 68 per 1,000.
Piper urged the Board to visit these houses of the poor because
he believed that 'more benefit would *accrue* from these inspec-
tions than from volumes of official reports'. Good water was still
not available in most of the streets and courts of the poor. The
burial ground was still open and more overcrowded than
ever. The river Skerne had been thoroughly cleaned but would
still be a menace to health while it carried all the town's
sewage. The town's lodging houses, however, had 'certainly
improved'. Piper had condemned these in 1851 as 'amongst the
greatest sources of evil', diseases being continually imported into
the town by 'tramping tinkers, pedlars, drovers, wandering
fiddlers', and the like. Now they had been put under police
control and the overcrowding limited, so that each lodger had
'250 cubic feet of air'. The other great advance of this year was
the Park. As Piper commented 'you have wisely and with much
taste laid out several acres of ground in the vicinity for the
recreation of the working classes.'

1854

By 1854 the really major improvements were coming. The
Board's big plan for a complete system of sewers was nearly
88 finished. 'Drains of scientific construction now *ramify* through-

out a great portion of the town,' so that 'before the close of the present year Darlington will in all probability be thoroughly drained'. Piper was also pleased that at last the 'surcharged burial ground of the Parish Church will be closed and water will be supplied to all the yards, courts and alleys'. Water could be supplied in this way because the Board had bought up the Darlington Gas and Water Company for £54,000. Piper was also enormously relieved that the cholera had not hit Darlington—'tho' the *inscrutable* pestilence raged within a few miles it has again left us *unscathed.*' He put this down to a rigorous policy of house to house visiting in 'the parts of the town where disease was known formerly to prevail'. In spite of all these improvements Piper was still worried by the number of people who died from diseases of the lungs. He urged the need for better ventilation in the houses of the working classes. He also suggested the need to get rid of the many slaughter-houses which were still in the town.

1855

The report for 1855 is the last of this series which Piper wrote. In it he reports that there had been a 'striking change in the sanitary condition of the town'. The population was evidently growing fast. There were 284 deaths that year but 514 births, a hundred more than the previous year. Only 2 cases of typhus were recorded and 'in the lowlying district east of the Skerne the death rate has fallen from 68 to 23 per 1,000'—a clear proof that better drainage could stop disease. But Piper evidently wanted the Board to guard against being too pleased with what had been done. 'Still there is much to do and more to undo.' 'Mortality amongst the children of the poor is still truly appalling' and more than one third of all deaths that year were of infants less than a year old. The Board had made enormous improvements to the public facilities in the town with sewers, water, baths, a park, a new burial ground, but now they were up against the problem of the houses themselves. Again Piper saw the problem clearly. 'The most difficult obstacle now is to remedy the present faulty construction of the dwellings of the working classes.' This attack on the overcrowding and insanitary state of private property was a much more complicated job because it was more difficult to interfere with private property. It was a problem which would keep the Board of Health busy for the rest of the century and beyond.

Results
Piper ends this report with a proud boast. 'Few Boards have effected more substantial improvements than that which I have the honour of addressing, the work of reformation which was so much needed has been carried out in earnest.' Finally, in a telling sentence, he writes: 'It is but an act of self-defence; for the rich man who lives in a comfortable and luxurious home, must keep in mind that his mansion cannot be safe, when the dark and filthy hovel breeds pestilence beside it.'

It was through the unsung efforts of local Boards of Health such as Darlington's that the quality of life of the poor was really improved. This improvement was made possible by the Public Health Act. Whatever the political fate of the Act its solid achievement can be found in the *archives* of the nearly 200 Local Boards which were set up under it. These archives have never been studied systematically, so we cannot know how many Boards were as vigorous as Darlington's. The total of improvements under these Boards may, however, have been considerable.

9 Chadwick's Downfall and Achievement

The End of the Board of Health

By 1854, in spite of the success of the Board of Health up and down the country, it had made a lot of enemies. Chadwick knew this and explained the situation in a letter to a friend. 'Our Board is *terminable* next year: powerful parties are labouring to prevent its renewal, and most probably they will prevent its renewal under any conditions on which I can be employed.' He goes on to list the 'strong interests' working against him, that is, the various groups of people who wanted to stop his work. There were 'the water companies who command some eighty votes; representatives of vestries whose administration we condemned, and from whom we proposed to take power; a powerful body of Parliamentary agents, from whom it is complained we have taken much business, and in the case of 157 towns (where the Act was applied) have done for hundreds of pounds that for which they would have obtained thousands. The water companies have retained two thirds of the leading journals (newspapers) in the Metropolis, which are writing personally and bitterly against me. I have been compelled to thwart Mr. Walter, the proprietor of 'The Times', and I have that journal against me. We have, moreover, been obliged to excite a strong landlord interest against us, in unwholesome houses, which we could not but condemn, and thus threaten those landlords, as they conceive, with expenses.' And so the catalogue goes on.

In July 1854, when the Government introduced a Bill to continue the Board of Health for a further two years, only bringing it directly under the control of the Home Secretary, all Chadwick's enemies joined forces, and after a bitter debate, the

Government was defeated by 74 votes to 65. The Board of Health had been overthrown. Next morning, in a leading article, 'The Times' jeered with delight.

'We prefer to take our chance of cholera and the rest than be bullied into health.

'There is nothing a man so hates as being cleaned against his will, or having his floors swept, his walls whitewashed, his pet dungheaps cleared away, or his thatch forced to give way to slate, all at the command of a sort of sanitary *bombailiff*. It is a positive fact that many have died of a good washing. All this shows the extreme tenderness with which the work of purification should advance. Not so thought Mr. Chadwick. New mops wash clean, thought he, and he set to work, everywhere washing and splashing, and twirling and rinsing, and sponging and sopping, and soaping and mopping, till mankind began to fear a deluge of soap and water. It was a perpetual Saturday night, and Master John Bull was scrubbed, and rubbed, and small-tooth-combed, till the tears came into his eyes, and his teeth chattered, and his fists clinched themselves with worry and pain.

'The truth is, Mr. Chadwick has very great powers, but it is not so easy to say what they can be applied to. Perhaps a retiring pension, with nothing to do, will be a less exceptionable mode of rewarding this gentleman, than what is called an active sphere.'

Chadwick's Retirement

In fact, that is exactly what happened to Chadwick. He was given a retiring pension of £1,000 a year and at the age of 54 he was prematurely retired. He lived another 36 years, but was never given another job. He retired to a cottage in Richmond, and kept himself busy writing a stream of pamphlets for learned Societies, and even stood, unsuccessfully, for Parliament. In his forced retirement he must have watched with great bitterness the slow progress in public health over the next fifteen years.

92

Slow Progress in Public Health

Although a revised Board of Health continued on a yearly basis for another four years, it was abolished in 1858. This really meant the end of the Government's attempts to interfere actively in the nation's health. Chadwick's greatest achievement had been to establish the idea of public health, but in putting that idea into practice, the Board of Health had tried to do too much too quickly, and the middle class voters had refused to be 'bullied into health'. They were not yet ready to pay for the health of the labouring classes.

In its place, in 1858, the Government appointed a Medical Officer, under the Privy Council, who had no power to act, but only to 'enquire and report'. The first medical officer was John Simon, and over the next twelve years he and a small team of medical officers did just that. They made a series of detailed investigations into every aspect of the nation's health. These reports, and Simon's own Annual Reports, gradually persuaded the public that more must be done about public health. In 1866,

John Simon

a new Sanitary Act was introduced which widened the definition of 'nuisances' and for the first time imposed on local authorities the 'duty' to do something about them. But this Act hardly made any difference because there was no central authority to compel them to act. At last, in 1871, this problem, too, was solved with the Local Government Act. Under this Act, a new Board was set up with responsibility for both Poor Law administration and public health. There was now a central authority again with an army of officials to carry on the struggle to make Great Britain a healthier place to live in. A new Public Health Act, which put into one law all the recent legislation, was passed in 1875 and from this time progress was much more rapid.

Chadwick's Achievement

Chadwick lived on to see these things happen. By now he had become a Grand Old Man, the father of the 'Sanitary Idea.' He was knighted at last in 1889 and given a public banquet.

'On Saturday, 2nd March,' reported the 'Illustrated London News', 'the veteran poor law reformer, civil servant and sanitary reformer, whose labours would have sufficed for three ordinary men was entertained at a dinner to congratulate him, not only on his birthday, but on his having received —why not a peerage?—the honour of promotion to the order of KCB from the Queen.'

When he died a year later, on July 6th 1890, even 'The Times' was warm in his praise.

'To the last, Sir Edwin Chadwick was a familiar figure at his club, and many an *habitué* of the Athenaeum will miss the benevolent and *leonine* face, wrinkled with the lines of thought, and surmounted by the black skull-cap. His features, as they well might, wore an expression of serene complacency; for it has been given to few men to do more or better work in his own special departments.

'Figures and undeniable facts were the *talismans* with which he accomplished achievements which to the contemporaries of his early manhood would have seemed miraculous. He may be said to have been the father of Modern Sanitary Science.'

Edwin Chadwick (left) photographed in his old age with two friends

Chadwick may have been arrogant and difficult to deal with, but he was one of the very few people in the nineteenth century, who permanently affected for the better, the way people lived. Let us leave the last word to his great successor, John Simon, who summed up Chadwick's career like this.

'In the earlier stages of Mr. Chadwick's career, when the essence of his work was to force public attention to the broad facts and consequences of a great public neglect, it mattered little whether he possessed the quality of judicial patience; but in his subsequent position of authority demands for the exercise of that virtue were great and constant. He perhaps did not sufficiently recognise that the case was one in which deliberate national consents had to be

95

obtained. He probably hoped to achieve in a few years the results which not ten times his few years could see achieved. But Mr. Chadwick, beyond any man of his time, knew what large fresh additions of human misery were accruing each day under the then almost universal prevalence of sanitary neglect. To those services of Mr. Chadwick's, we of this nation unquestionably owe that our statesmen of those times were first awakened to the duty of caring for the Public Health, and that the first endeavours were made to bring Health under the protection of Law.'

How Do We Know?

Chadwick left a vast collection of his papers, and these are in the library of University College, London. Most people, however, will be able to get all the information they need from S. E. Finer's superb biography 'The Life and Times of Edwin Chadwick' (Methuen). This is a long book, but it has very full quotations from Chadwick's private papers.

The amount of information on the Poor Laws and Public Health is enormous. Both the Poor Law Commissioners and the General Board of Health published annual reports and these should be available in the better reference libraries. There you should also find the published reports of the Royal Commission on the Poor Laws (1832) and, Chadwick's 'Report on the Sanitary condition of the Labouring Population' (1842) and his supplement on 'Interment in Towns' (1843).

Local Boards of Guardians and Boards of Health (where they were set up) were required to keep full records and many of these have been preserved. The chapters on Stow Union and Darlington were both written from local records and you may find similar collections in your local Record Office or Public Library.

Things To Do

Because the Poor Laws and Public Health affected every town and village they make ideal subjects for local projects. Either in groups or as a class, you can discover how they affected your own town or village, and write up your results as a permanent record. Here are some general hints on sources.

The Poor Law

1. The Guardians had to keep minute books in which they recorded what was decided at every meeting. These will probably be preserved and your teacher may be able to arrange for you to study them at your local Record Office, Public Library, or Town Clerk's Office.

2. There is quite a chance that the Workhouse may still exist, though usually it will have been added to or even rebuilt later in the nineteenth century. The hospital is the most likely building to look at. Try to arrange a guided tour of the building if you find it, and make a rough plan of its layout.

3. The public library may have copies of your local newspaper for this period. Read the papers which cover the time when your Union was formed for reports of any rioting or disturbances.

4. Many old people still remember the days of the Workhouse. Try to find some who were in it and make tape-recordings of what they remember. Interview several people so that you can compare their comments.

Public Health

1. If your town was one which set up a local Board of Health under the 1848 Act, its minutes may also have been preserved and will provide just as much detailed information as the Guardians minutes. There is a list of these towns in Brockington, 'Public Health in the Nineteenth Century' (Livingstone).

2. Even if there are no records in your area you will probably be able to get a lot of information from people such as your Medical Officer of Health or the Borough Surveyor. Try to get one of them to come and tell you how public health is organised in your town.

3. Get your teacher to organise trips to your local Water Board, Sewage Farm and Cemetery. Write up accounts of how they are organised and compare these with the accounts of how things were.

Glossary

accrue, to grow from
aggregate, a sum total
aloof, at a distance
archives, historical records
assail, to attack
attorney, old name for a lawyer
bombailiff, a bailiff of the lowest sort, used in making arrests
bureaucracy, rule by Government officials
capricious, changing their minds for no reason
cesspool, well to take the refuse from lavatories
clandestinely, secretly
Commissioner, member of a Government Board
contagious, passed on by contact
contaminating, making impure
copious, plentiful
deporting, sent abroad as a punishment, often to Australia
designated, called
dispersion, breaking up
disrepute, bad reputation
eminence, rising ground, a hill
enumerated, made a list of
exasperation, anger
extricated, got free
fanatical, filled with excessive enthusiasm for something
filter beds, pond or tank used to filter water
flag, pave with flagstones
forbearance, restraint
habitué, one who has the habit of going often to a place
improvidence, taking no care for the future
infringement, attack upon
inscrutable, mysterious
intimation, notice
inundated, flooded with water
laissez-faire, letting things alone
leonine, like a lion

molestation, attack

nauseous, disgusting

opulence, wealth

outdoor relief, poor relief given outside the workhouse

overseer, the official who had to look after relief for the poor

pauper, a poor person, receiving poor-law relief

polluted, filthy

poor rates, money paid by householders to support the poor

porous, with tiny holes through which water can seep

prejudicial, causing damage to

premature, before the proper time

privy, lavatory

probationary ward, ward into which paupers were put while awaiting examination

putrefying, rotting

ramify, spread into a number of branches

refractory ward, special cell for rebellious paupers

remedial measures, suggestions for making the situation better

repealed, cancelled

respiratory system, parts of the body used in breathing

sabre, cavalry sword with a curved blade

seat, place of residence

select committee, a small committee of Parliament for special investigations

sinister, corrupt

skillee, thin watery porridge made from oatmeal

stigmatise, blacken the name of

sundered, separated

talisman, something by which extraordinary results are achieved

terminable, liable to be ended

unanimously, all in agreement

unscathed, uninjured

utility, rightness

vicinity, neighbourhood

water closet, a lavatory which is flushed by water